THE MEDICAL OFFICER'S DIARY
RAF LÜNEBURG 1947

THE MEDICAL OFFICER'S DIARY RAF LÜNEBURG 1947

Flt. Lt. Richard Harrison

edited by
Peter Harrison and Vivian Foster

MENIN HOUSE

Menin House Publishers,
an imprint of Tommies Guides Military Booksellers & Publishers

Gemini House
136–140 Old Shoreham Road
Brighton
BN3 7BD

First published in Great Britain by
Menin House 2017

For more information please visit
www.tommiesguides.co.uk

A catalogue record for this book is available
from the British Library

ISBN 978-1-908336-26-2

Cover design by Ryan Gearing
Typeset by Vivian@Bookscribe

Printed and bound in Great Britain

This book is dedicated to all

Richard Harrison's patients

Richard Harrison M.B., B.S.

*"It would be a shame if the Harrisons went down into silence
without leaving their mark on Farringdon Street!*

*I expect you'll have wondered at the writing on the script
the old man is reading. The former Judge Advocate General
of Hamburg, who is at the moment frying chicken for my
tea, says the quotation is one Freidrich Ruckert, a German
philosopher and broadly translated means: 'A good book is
worth a second reading: only a good book should ever be read
even once.'*

*Well, here comes that chicken so, for the present,
Yours aye...."*

FOREWORD

Richard Harrison, who died in 2009, was a distinguished orthopaedic surgeon at Furness General Hospital, Barrow in Furness. He qualified in Medicine in 1944, with a distinction in obstetrics, at St Bartholomew's Hospital Medical School, London, during the second World War. In those wartime days, medical students were deferred from military service until after qualification and a period of training in civilian hospitals in junior posts until being called up for service in one or other of the armed services.

In due course, Richard was inducted into the medical branch of the Royal Air Force in 1946, by which time the war was over, but British forces were still widely scattered overseas. After preliminary training, Richard was posted to the Royal Air Force (RAF) station at Lüneburg, in the British Zone of occupied Germany. He was a dedicated letter-writer and photographer; this book presents his diaries and many of his black and white photographs taken that year, the year of his marriage.

After his military service, Richard resumed his surgical training, which led to his consultant appointment in Barrow in Furness. He retained his interest in military medicine and became a major in the Royal Army Medical Corps Territorial Army, serving with the Airborne Forces. He was awarded the Territorial Decoration and was appointed officer of the Order of St John. His diary, reproduced in these pages, provides us with a vivid account of a military doctor's life in occupied Europe during those bleak post-war years. The text is fully illustrated by the profuse output of this enthusiastic amateur photographer.

This is a book that will be read with great interest, I am sure, by a wide audience of doctors and their families, by service and ex-service families and by all who are interested in the life and times of those hectic and bleak years, with the 'Cold War', with what was then the USSR, just in the offing.

Prof. Harold Ellis, CBE
27 September 2016

HAROLD ELLIS

Harold Ellis was born in Whitechapel, London in 1926. He qualified in medicine at Oxford in 1948. He trained in surgery in Oxford, Sheffield, Northampton and London, spending 1950–52 as a surgical specialist in the Royal Army Medical Corps. He was appointed the foundation Professor of Surgery at Westminster Medical School, University of London in 1962 and remained there until his retirement in 1989. Since then he has taught Anatomy, first at Cambridge and, since 1993, at Guy's. He is the author of twenty-seven books on Anatomy, Surgery and Medical History. In 1987 he was appointed the CBE.

(photo courtesy of King's College London)

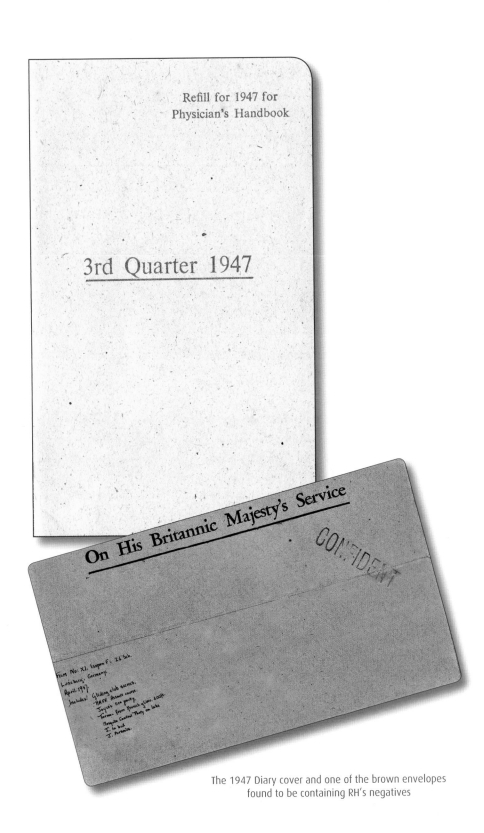

Refill for 1947 for
Physician's Handbook

3rd Quarter 1947

On His Britannic Majesty's Service

CONFIDENT

From No: XI. 150pm F: 26 Sch.
Luncburg; Germany.
April 1947
Includes: Gliding club scenes.
RAFK Absent course.
Joyce Eco party.
Terrace from french offices. 800fs.
Margate Sontra; Party on lake
J. in bed
J. Portrain.

The 1947 Diary cover and one of the brown envelopes
found to be containing RH's negatives

PREFACE

My father, Richard Harrison, was a surgeon. Abetted by my mother, Joyce, their large house in Cumbria had become the depository of eighty years' of accumulated memorabilia. In 2009, having been "served notice of his own mortality", he confirmed to me the whereabouts of funds to ensure my mother's future welfare. He reluctantly admitted that the task of clearing the substantial family home in the Lake District might pose a challenge. I was instructed that a local house clearer should be retained to remove and dispose of the content: "without undue sentimentality, only keeping a few souvenirs of personal interest." He died soon afterwards.

Acting upon the professional advice of a gentleman auctioneer, the last instruction to employ a house clearer was not fulfilled. A team of four and on some days, six, careful individuals sifted through every item in the house for sixteen days before the property was empty and ready to sell. Even without any sentimental consideration the task was onerous and dusty. Endless boxes to be opened, sorted and frequently consigned to a bonfire that was not extinguished for a fortnight. Six thousand books were removed for sale elsewhere. Skips collected from the drive and medical records of more than half a century properly destroyed. By the end of those weeks a certain recklessness had set in. It became a somewhat arbitrary decision whether to toss a packing case onto the bonfire or to place it in a safe place for later investigation or donation to a museum. We'll never know what curios or documents went up in flames. This is the story of a very dull cardboard box that was transported to my attic in East Sussex where it remained unopened until a wet Easter weekend in 2013.

Spring 2013 – The Box

Items removed from that house shared an unusual quality. Anyone handling them became coated in a slightly abrasive dust that left the fingers slightly sore and the lungs a little congested. The auctioneer called the latter "Sale Room Cough". Having resolved never to leave my own executors exposed to the same trials, I took it upon myself to clear, or at least identify, the inherited boxes now in my own attic. A miserably cold Easter weekend and its ensuing boredom led me up the attic ladder to start work. My

application to the task was minimal and I soon became engrossed in a long forgotten collection of my old Matchbox cars. I tired of even that and resolved to consign something to the tip. The most likely candidate being a very tatty cardboard box clearly bursting with very many identical brown envelopes. I took this to my small office and inspected it in a better light. I'd guessed that those envelopes, there were 107 of them, might contain negative films. Previous experience had long resigned me to the assumption that these would prove to be clinical images – usually of deformed hands and hips.

A quick dip into the first brown envelope yielded the first film strip which was easily scanned onto my computer. Unmistakeably a nicely composed forest scene with, at its centre, a derelict German Panther tank with my father astride it! I wasn't surprised, I'd been brought up on tales of my parents' life in Germany in 1947 as part of the Army of Occupation. What I'd never known about or even seen were the photographs of that time. During that Easter weekend I started to view those photographs and I realised that I'd lifted the lid of my family's Pandora's Box. In those envelopes marked "Germany" were six hundred and thirty two images. The most interesting pictures were passed around family and friends. Each of the envelopes had been labelled with date, film type and exposure and a brief description of the subjects captured. That left a tantalising gap between the picture described and the actual story of its participants and what happened next. My brother Richard's attic started to yield many of the answers, Despite his avowed intent not to be inundated with boxes of moribund family papers, he had carefully kept a box of diaries. It was now apparent that Dad had been a diligent and fluent writer since the age of ten. What had been a picture of a derelict tank in a German forest now became part of a scene in which suspicious locals eyed well dressed strangers. The narrative had started…

Rose at 10.30hrs & breakfasted as usual – had an emergency call at 1115hrs saying that the Liberty run to Hamburg had overturned at Winsen. Foulds picked me up in one of the ambulances – we did 55mph most of the way, & arrived at the scene at about 1150hrs. Found the 3-ton Thorneycroft lying on its side – it had originally turned upside down after a skid – and one badly shocked man with a back injury still by the roadside. Sent him to the 94TH BMH and then proceeded to the nearby German hospital. Here – in a very shabby dirty little establishment in a side street – we found the body of a Corporal – dead with a compound shattered # of the mandible and probably, a fractured base : a case of fractured ribs, a laceration of thigh, broken arm & a fourth man – If..., one of our old thorns in the side on Sick Parade – with a # upper 1/3 of femur. Our ministrations mostly devolved into injections of morphine & a rapid despatch to Hamburg. Then we moved the body to the mortuary & I returned to Luneberg, passing two more cases en route for the 94TH as I did so.

Rest of the day quiet – I developed some films I'd taken during the morning & tonight Foulds came down & stayed overnight – out what chat went on until the wee sma' hours.

THE MAMMOTH TASK OF HOUSE CLEARING

INTRODUCTION

'There's Old Dick and Young Dick
and Young Dick's Son
And Young Dick will be Old Dick
When Old Dick's done'

Since 1810 the first sons of the Harrison family have been named Richard. On the 8 July 1922 my father Richard Harrison joined the line. His father , Richard (of course) had returned four years earlier from The Western Front with a Major's crown on each shoulder. He'd left for France as a Trooper.

Young Richard demonstrated a precocious talent for the Science subjects at Mill Hill (the school that had already nurtured Crick, discoverer of DNA). Aged seventeen at the outbreak of the Second World War, he'd already secured a place to study Medicine at St. Bartholomew's Hospital. The Blitz rapidly necessitated the evacuation of the Medical School to Cambridge. Richard found himself digs in the company of fellow medical student Alex Comfort who was later to write *The Joy of Sex*.

Having achieved a 'Distinction' in his studies, the young doctor gained his first experiences of surgery and trauma in the East End of London during the final V1 and V2 storms of the war. Enduring the same hardships was an attractive and well educated BBC assistant, Joyce Masters, working at Broadcasting House. The day after her participation in the VJ day broadcast they announced their engagement. On 22 June 1946 they married. Richard packed fourteen books in his honeymoon suitcase.

Their bliss was short lived. Richard was called up and commissioned into the RAF as a Medical Officer. A short and relatively painless induction course at RAF Cheddington was followed by his posting to France in The Rhone 'G' Chain (a descendant of the very secret 'Oboe' Radar system) at Lodève.

From this undemanding location Richard started his photography and continued his daily correspondence not only to Joyce but also his father, stepmother and his three siblings: Tim, Alice and Pam. Joyce soon made her way to France and an idyllic life of mountain scenery, culture and fine cuisine awaited. Richard's letter home reflects the inevitable outcome.

On 30 November it was reported that Air Marshall Bennett in Paris had 'expressed horror at the idea of 180 men having their own MO in Lodève.'

By 5 December, RH was ordered to report to BAFO Germany 'forthwith' and Joyce returned alone to London (having declined a job offer as governess to the family of a Vicomtesse in Montpelier). The long train journey took him across war torn Europe and deep into the remains of the Reich. 151 Repair Unit (Aircraft) was without a Medical Officer following a fatal flying accident. Richard was installed in his own room within the Station Sick Quarters, RAF Lüneburg before Christmas.

This former Luftwaffe airfield had been the home of the illustrious Kampfgeschwader 26 (KG 26) 'Löwengeschwader', the 'Lion Wing' after its insignia. The airfield and its buildings had been built on a grand scale, to last. (The 'Lion' motif still abundant in 2015. Ed.)

We join Dick Harrison as he completes his diary that 25 December 1946.

Wednesday, 25 December 1946

Rose at 10.00 hrs and spent the morning reading and writing a letter to Mr & Mrs Masters. At 12.20 hrs I started serving the Xmas dinners to our two patients (tonsillitis : shingles) and to my staff plus the German ancillaries – about 20 in all. We had an excellent meal, in the middle of which G/Cpt. Walker arrived on a visit of inspection, which was however, short. Then we all had an 'international' sing-song, completed with 'Lilli Marlene' from the German driver who had been put in one-man U boats as a military punishment. Followed by 'Heilige Nacht' and similar numbers; everyone on terms of the utmost good fellowship.

Went round to the Browns for tea and got rather bored. At 19.15 hrs to the Mess for a semi-formal dinner, my first in the service. After dinner there was to have been a party, but not many turned up and the evening degenerated into a drinking session and a sing-song which was the greater failure because ladies were present.

As an offset to this, I contacted our Allied Military Government official about a microscope and the PSI officer about some cigarettes. As I prepared to leave I was summoned to see two German servants, both hopeless drunk and both unpleasantly sick, who were put to bed in the batman's quarters. On which cheerful note a not-too-bad Xmas day ended at approximately 02.00 hrs.

CHRISTMAS 1946 LÜNEBURG SSQ

FRANCE 1946

think you will like

work and, with a warm

R
Dext

JANUARY 1947

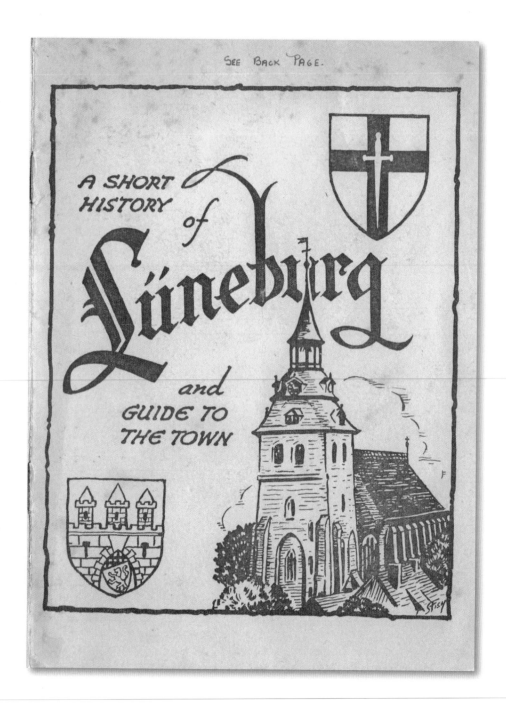

SEE BACK PAGE.

A SHORT HISTORY of Lüneburg and GUIDE TO THE TOWN

Street Plan of Lüneburg

Printed by Printing and Stationery Service, 30 Corps District

JANUARY 1947

Saturday, 4 January
Short sick parade – then took our ambulance down to Lüneburg and, with the assistance of our dispenser, Monica, ordered some photographic enlargements and bought some surgical instruments – notably a very fine saw (48 marks).

Uneventful afternoon … snow on the ground – partially thawing – and weather bitterly cold.

Sunday, 5 January
Did not get up till 10.10hrs. A fine day but bitterly cold. I spent most of it writing and reading, but had one call out – to a man with a malarioid response to tonsillitis, this evening.

Listened to 'Mutiny on the Bounty' on the radio tonight and, soon after, to 'Time for Verse'.

Lüneburg airfield control tower

Lüneburg (Am Stintmarkt)

Tuesday, 7 January

Still bitterly cold. A mild case of frost-bitten toes this morning … this afternoon I did a TABC inoculation for a Malcolm Club girl – mostly in the hopes of getting a coffee from them.

The NCO i/c, Williams, very bossily taking over the reins today and he is quite obviously the male counterpart of some hospital sisters I have met.

Letters from Joyce and Tim – who says he had most of his kit stolen in Cairo, poor chap.

Wednesday, 8 January

A very dull day – warmer, but elsewhere in the camp the water supply has failed. Even my knowledge of water dowsers is now being called upon! Tried to contact CQG about my microscope, but Stanmers, my contact, has shot off on leave for two weeks.

Thursday, 9 January

Quiet day – still have the organization of diphtheria immunization as my chief problem. I went down into town today and bought some more surgical instruments – I am rapidly collecting a most impressive array. Today's items included a couple of beautiful chisels and a fine amputation knife.

Spent a very absorbing half hour in the mess today catching up with all Tim's letters home, which Dad has forwarded. Even the old Sam Browne has now gone west, alas! But I feel it played it's most important part that night when we all saw Tim wearing it for the first time.

Lüneburg airfield (Anson)

Friday, 10 January

Went down to the airfield this morning and had tea in Flying Control. Then back to see a casualty – man slightly cut on the nose by a starting handle which flew off a compressor.

'Married families' this afternoon – sore throats and bronchitis – and this evening just read in the Mess. Paddy Goodman, the ambulance driver, brought some more surgical instruments back from Hamburg for me this evening.

Post-prandial stupor, Officers' Mess, 13.30 hours

Sunday, 12 January

This has been a very dull, boring weekend. Things started badly on Saturday morning when my 'clock repairs' were collected, but films were not ready because there had been a fire in the shop. I tried to swap some cigarettes for a camera and failed because the instrument was not there – though I may be able to obtain it tomorrow. Spent most of the day reading, writing letters and listening to the radio.

Monday, 13 January

A lengthy sick parade … slush and mud makes the Hamburg road indescribably bleak to me today.

Today did a bit more 'Black', buying an ex-German army surgical case in lovely leather, for 250 cigarettes (see Appendix 1 – The Bollman Case).

Tuesday, 14 January

Checked orderly room staff for Scarlatina today – and tonight was told of a Smallpox case, which – with a little trepidation – I hastened down to see. Cold, slushy evening, which I spent organizing quarantine measures amongst the Dienstgruppen, and laying on vaccine for tomorrow.

This evening – in between rushing around – did a lumbar puncture (eventually successfully) on a man brought in comatose without any PS save for a slight neck rigidity. The fluid was clear – what is the matter with him?

Very thrilled with my first case of Variola – but hope it is also my last. Have been looking at my vaccination marks tonight, and wish I felt surer that last scratch at Marsworth had been effective.

Lüneburg Rathaus (Town Hall) which was also used as a VD Clinic

ON ACTIVE SERVICE LETTER FORM

151 Rua   *15 January 1947*
BAFO
BAOR

Dear Dad,

The weather here has improved today, deep snow earlier in the week gradually gave way to equally deep slush and ice, so we've been cut off for a bit. However, the thaw is well advanced now and all our roads open again.

Thank you for the 'Synopsis' (ed. a medical reference book) which arrived safely yesterday – just in time. The previous day, Monday, we had the usual dreary Monday morning sick parade – about thirty bods with SFA between them. Then the last chap took off his shirt – Scarlet Fever. So, what with quarantines etc. Monday was a busy day.

Yesterday I began to feel that things were getting organized, despite the fact that the bad road state had made it necessary to retain the case here. Did I but know it, things were just starting. At five-thirty in the afternoon I saw SMALLPOX for the first time. Talk about Panic! Within five minutes R.H. from a humble F/O, became the most important single officer in Lüneburg. I was given a big staff car and powers of a Unit Commander, I spent all evening from then on stopping troop movements, posting guards, and laying on vaccines. I attended a Staff Officers' conference this morning, and am now waiting with bated breath for Case Two. The first one was a German POW – it has been confirmed by two German doctors in the local hospital. I feel very pleased at having see one – after reading about it so often, it's quite a thrill: and makes me, I feel, one of quite a small clique of doctors!

2

(ed. Smallpox was so rare in the UK that hospitals kept a register of doctors who had seen the disease and were thus able to diagnose it.)

Lymph has arrived here this afternoon and we start vaccinating 750 contacts this evening. Little Dickey will be first on the list, I assure you!

This afternoon another F/O Medical has arrived (Thomas J. M.– Guy's). I hope that this does not bode another move for me. It's alright for now of course, but if another MO is needed in BAFO this station will have to manage on one. And – since Thomas has four months seniority to me – the individual detached would be me. For the moment he becomes Unit MO whilst I, knowing more about the local geography, am O.C. Variola!

I'm sending sometime, an ex-Luftwaffe MO's case which I bought completely fitted out. It may well get 'lost' in the Customs so I have stripped it of its fittings and am retaining them. If it gets through it makes a beautiful visiting bag – if not – well the instruments are worth the seven bob anyhow.

(ed. A large proportion of RH's letters deal with the despatch of German medical instruments, bought or bartered, intended for use in private practice after demobilization. This was before the NHS.)

P.S. Have vaccinated myself tonight.
D.

Friday, 17 January

Warmer – and quieter – day. Vaccinations of odd families today and nothing of undue event. Made one trip into Lüneburg, and had a look round my wards on my return. Pleurisy case now seems to have turned into a definite but slightly atypical pneumonia. Faring pretty well with my new colleague. Tonight had an 'hour on the books' for the first time since reaching Germany.

Lüneburg   *17 January 1947*

Dear Dad,

A short note only, to say I am hale and hearty, rather hard worked – no, we have not had an influx of smallpox cases, but the prophylactic measures have kept me on my toes ever since my last letter. I've done several hundred vaccinations, and some idea of the administrative job imposed upon me can be gathered from the fact that, as I learn from the Exchange today, Station Sick Quarters handled 525 incoming calls alone in the 24 hours ending last night!

The worst business was last night – at lunchtime yesterday I discovered that a 'contact' had left before the quarantine was imposed and was off to the UK on leave. I immediately phoned the Hook of Holland and had him detained at the Embarkation Point. At 20.00 hrs last night the M.O. there phoned back to say he was holding the entire leave train – some 400 bods! – and the corresponding boat. Nor would he release it on my authority alone. So from then until 23.40 hrs – entirely and literally – I was on the phone ('Number One Priority'!)

D.

Saturday, 18 January

Sick parade this morning – seems to be an increasing number of upper respiratory tract infections and I begin to wonder if I am treating the chaps too leniently.

Went down to Lüneburg and spent a few more of my marks on surgical instruments – I only wish I could find a shop with a really good stock, because I could spend marks almost literally like water.

An hour on 'skins' tonight, which I find more interesting as I learn more about them.

This evening went down to Horrock's Theatre… saw a farce 'See How They Run' which was too farcical to be amusing. Back to SSQ, gave a tubunic to my case with pneumonia, who has a good deal of pain tonight; talked with the staff and so to bed.

Sunday, 19 January

Listened to 'Programme Parade' as I ate my breakfast – my usual practice on days when I haven't got my current *Radio Times*: then turned over again and slept until just after 10.00hrs.

Spent this morning doing some 'skins' and writing letters. At lunch time I received current *Lancets* etc. so I had plenty of reading matter to occupy me over the afternoon.

Only one call out in day – before dinner, to see a small girl with bronchitis. Rushed through my dinner tonight – some wild duck recently shot by my brother officers.

Monday, 20 January

Received my camera this morning – a virtually new 'Retina I' with which I am very well pleased. I now require only an exposure meter, some field glasses and a microscope and I will have reached my self-imposed quota!

Lüneburg   *20 January 1947*

Dear Dad,

I've been christening the camera this afternoon. We've had a 'Martinet' (twin-seater fighter trainer, resembles a 'Battle' on test, so we did a 'shoot up' of Lüneburg, the 'drome and Hamburg. I found it difficult to get good pictures because I nearly got blown out whenever I pushed the cowling back ... I had a very good look at the Hamburg dock area though, and at some of these famous submarine pens.

D.

Aerial view of Lüneburg

Tuesday, 21 January

The most interesting item today – after I had been round Lüneburg taking a few shots – was an hour's flight in a Martinet (drogue towing two-seater). We circled Lüneburg and the airfield at about 500–900 ft whilst I tried to take photos. Some of the results suffered from my reluctance to lean out of the cockpit to get good views when I had had to undo the safety harness in order to stand up! Have got at least one good picture though, I am well satisfied with all my ground efforts.

Wednesday, 22 January

To my surprise on awaking, found there had been a slight fall of snow overnight. Very slack day from a medical viewpoint.

A large parcel of 'Comforts' arrived today from home, quite safely.

I spent the evening (a) doing 'skins' and 'abstracts'; (b) developing another strip of film; (c) listening to Mystery Playhouse; (d) listening to the tail end of *Carmen* from France.

Friday, 24 January

A very bright afternoon – hung about waiting for an Auster lift, but missed the best of the sunlight. Nevertheless, I did manage to get in a session over Lüneburg and took half a dozen shots of the town and the airfield.

This evening I developed them. I was very gratified by the results, though I scratched the emulsion on a couple of exposures whilst drying the damn films! To bed very annoyed.

Saturday, 25 January

Busy morning – I took sick parade since F/O Thomas returned inebriated last night and did not feel up to it.

Went to Horrock's Theatre to see a variety show: some very good turns – notably a very German, very attractive, and ingenious marionette show. And a Japanese turn – juggling, spinning not a barrel, but a small boy with the feet of a woman swinging by her hair from her husband's teeth.

RAF Officer's Mess, Lüneburg

Sunday, 26 January

Worked and wrote letters all day, took a few snaps but less than I intended because it became bitterly cold so quickly.

This evening spent almost four hours printing snaps – for the most part unsuccessfully … due to a poor contact between film and paper. To bed very tired about 02.00 hrs.

Tuesday, 28 January

Sick parade as usual all day – went to Lüneburg this afternoon and took some pictures about town. Returned in time to stitch up an airman whose face was gashed when a tow rope parted between two lorries.

Did a couple of hours pathology today and developed a film strip tonight – am still consistently pleased with my negatives but not so happy about the finished prints.

SSQ Ambulance in the snow

Wednesday, 29 January

One of my quietest days for a couple of weeks – bitterly cold but periods of bright sunshine. Went down to Lüneburg and bought a few odd souvenirs – shield, brooches, miniature dolls – this morning. Spent this afternoon reading and revising.

Listening to 'Grimm's Fairy Tale' and 'The Man Who Wasn't There' in the Mystery Playhouse series, and so to bed.

Thursday, 30 January

After sick parade this morning had quite a shock when I was told I must go to Paris to attend a Court of Enquiry – I can only presume that it is upon the 'Chalky Jeep Smash'.

04.35 hrs was called by the duty orderly – would I go down to see Mrs R. Half suspecting the trouble, I went down and found the good woman, bless her, sitting up in bed, physically fit and obviously recovering from a row with her husband, to conclude which she apparently had a fainting fit.

30 January 1947

Dear Dad,

I presume the Inquiry is on a jeep incident that happened the week after Joyce joined me – we were both going to Avignon and Carpentras, with the F/O i/c 108 AMES, who was driving with more zeal than discretion. Whilst taking a sharp corner just outside Montpelier at about 50 mph he lost control and/or due to a tyre blow out. We went off the road and stopped a little violently on a steep bank. The F.O's wife was concussed a bit, everyone else was all right and Joyce was as cool as a cucumber – strolled off to a nearby village and rang Lodeve for a tow and an ambulance. I don't suppose she showed you the quite interesting photographs I took during the few minutes after the prang. Anyhow the jeep was a 'write off' and I suppose they're trying to pin the blame on the F/O – which, truth to tell, is quite right. Still, I can't say as much in Paris !

RH Jeep Crash November 22 1946. Mrs W visible lying on the roadside, suffering from shock. J & Chalky have left to summon assistance. [The vehicle has been 'winterized' unofficially with a plywood canopy]

Joyce talking to Mrs W who is now feeling better. Chalky filling in Accident Form.

'January 1947, Lüneburg, 09.28 for Hannover'

Friday, 31 January

Up at 08.30 hrs and down to Lüneburg station. Took a train from there about 09.30 hrs. and after a slightly chilly journey, arrived at Hannover 15 12.05 hrs. Here it was very cold indeed, and the shattered streets looked incredibly miserable. I had a few purchases to make though I was pleased to find a fair number of things to buy. The only regret was that I was down to the expedient of offering cigarettes, for I had left all my marks with one of the ambulance drivers.

This done I went in a 3-tonner (which I still dislike doing intensely) to the 'London Barracks' transit camp, just outside the city. There I had a poor lunch and a worse tea … At 17.00 hours another 3-tonner took me back to Hannover Station where I froze on the platform at intervals of suffocating in a warm, but very very odoriferous, latrine, until about 17.45 hrs when a beautifully hot empty train came in.

RIGHT: 'January 1947, Lüneburg. A chimney sweep on his bike.

Meanwh

think you will like

work and, with a warm

R

Desi

FEBRUARY 1947

FEBRUARY 1947

Saturday, 1 February
Dozed fairly soundly in the train until about 06.00 hrs. Then went along to the NAAFI bar and had a cup of coffee. Returned to my corner and dozed some more until we entered Brussels about 09.00 hrs … Then repaired to RAF movements and laid on a sleeper for tonight.

I spent the rest of the morning – which was fairly warm – ambling round the city. And, since I had no Belgian money at all and Brussels' chief claim to my interest was as a shopping centre, and since everything looked ferociously expensive, I did not find it too intriguing.

Eventually I exchanged 2/6d for 2D Frs. from a couple of RAF police, and with this, after lunch, I went to *Pour Qui Sonne les Cycles* at the local cinema. Found this less enthralling than when I first saw it – double subtitles in French and Flemish being a bit disturbing.

Sunday, 2 February
Reached Paris between 04.00–05.00 hrs. I was allowed to lie undisturbed until only 06.00 hrs, then I had to dress. Fortunately had a 20 Fr. note on me, left from my last visit to the capital, so I bought myself cups of the most tasty coffee I've ever tasted, and went to sleep full length on a bench in the crowded waiting room … Since the club was closed I went up to Arc de Triomphe, took some snaps, sold 50 cigarettes for 200 Frs. and rejected an offer of 10,000 for my gold chronometer … After lunch shot off to l'Opera-Comique and paid 175 Frs. for a seat under the impression I was going to see *Mignon* – actually it was, to my disgust, *Lakmé*, which I intensely disliked. (Anyhow, I've seen an opera in Paris now!)

This evening went to Hotel du Palais Royal and met the F/O who is holding the investigation – to my surprise, on some dangerous drugs missing from a batch sent to the Rhône Chaine.

L'Arc de Triomphe, Paris, with a smattering of snow

Monday, 3 February

Up at 07.45 hrs, had breakfast and went out in a converted 3-tonner to La Jonchère where I stayed till 14.00 hrs delivering myself of a long statement about the Thornycroft smash and worrying about possible errors and deficiencies in other D.Ds stored at Lodeve.

Tried to shake off my troubles this afternoon by dashing round the camera shops trying to buy colour filters etc., and being defeated by the cost. Bought a small silk handkerchief for Joyce and bumped into F/O Williams (of Mende) as I went for tea in the British Officer's Club.

Paris damp and a little chilly. Slushy snow on the ground not making for a cheerful scene and everything very expensive in the shops.

Hotel du Paris Royal
Paris
Mony 3.2.47

Dear Dad,

To let you know I am hale and hearty and have survived a lot of travelling. I'm writing this just before setting off on the Road Back to BAFO and will communicate more fully on arrival.

The Rhine Army train fell short of the Nord Express standard, on which I'd failed to get a reservation, and I had no sleeper. However, I made myself comfortable on a sleeper and fed in a NAAFI car. We got into Brussels about nine next morning, and I fed in a very good restaurant British Army Staff had taken over. When I'd exhausted the City's sights – and I'm getting to know Brussels by now – I went to the cinema and saw 'Pour Qui Sonne le Glos' (Hemmingway's 'For Whom…') a second time. Then trekked across to Gare du Midi and took the fast overnight train to Paris.

Yours aye,
Dick

Tuesday, 4 February
Had a good sleep on the train before we got into Brussels and I went straight to the Transit Restaurant for a shave and some breakfast.

Spent the afternoon, after reading in the restaurant, wandering round Brussels, buying some Angora skins for Joyce, a brooch for Alice and 2 kilos of coffee to take back to BAFO.

Boarded the train at 18.15 hrs … I've never spent a more uncomfortable night. I lay full length on a Pullman seat, cowering beneath my greatcoat, with my pyjamas wrapped about my feet and a towel round my head, feeling bitterly cold and waking from an uneasy doze at short intervals to peer at thick snow outside the window.

Paris Opera, La Bohème. Opening scene 'Café Momus'. RH went to great pains not to process the photograph back to front as you can see by the lettering on the glass.

Wednesday, 5 February

At 05.45 hrs after a terrible night staggered along to the NAAFI car and drank some tea and had a spam roll for breakfast. Then – much too late – found a warm seat in the 'Sgt. & W.O.'s' carriage and dozed there until we reached Hanover. Sat in the Red Shield Canteen and had cream cake for breakfast.

… Reached Lüneburg about 13.15 hrs. Had a hot bath in SSQ and a feast of accumulated mail – including a scarf and some handkerchiefs from a devoted wife.

Saturday, 8 February

Up at 08.40 hrs. Thomas suffering from a slight hangover so I took sick parade and then went down to Lüneburg in search of photographic accessories – quite unsuccessfully.

In the evening developed my 'Paris' films – somewhat disappointed by the results – (a) two double exposures, (b) the fact that 'La Bohème' shots are (save for those of 'Café Momus') very much under exposed.

Sunday, 9 February

Spent morning doing Path. and writing up odd notes … Very quiet and rather dull day.

Fuel situation seems to be bad in the UK – news bulletins are at present largely concerned with economies to be introduced etc. Out here it's cold, but not exceptionally so.

Monday, 10 February

Chilly but bright day, and very little work to do. Went down to Lüneburg this morning and spent 100 marks on some forceps etc. and a very useful box of scalpels.

This afternoon did a couple of hours' work on the books, at the end of which I was called to see a German who had been run over by a lorry but who had no external injuries to show for it.

The big item of the day was a note from J saying that she will travel on the 19th of this month and I immediately set about checking up the question of our living quarters.

Tuesday, 11 February

One of my quietest days to date … Bought a Meerschaum pipe for ½ lb coffee and 10 cigarettes from a charwoman here – alas, it is so old that it is only fit to hang on the wall!

Spent the latter period experimenting with an improvised enlarger, but had to go out at about 23.00 hrs to see a 'drunk' in the guard house – the returning liberty run from Lüneburg seemed to include a few more like him as well!

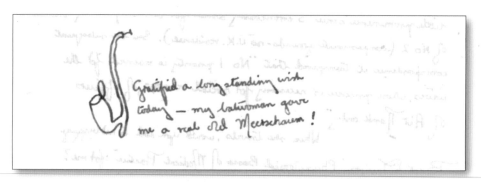

Wednesday, 12 February

Snow falling and settling all day. Very little work – I did some revision during both the morning and the afternoon and devoted the evening to trying a few more enlargements.

No mail in today – wrote a final letter to Joyce, and sent some snaps to Dad.

Thursday, 13 February

Quiet day – went down to Lüneburg this morning to negotiate for some film supplies. This afternoon down again to see a child with mumps. Did a little revision on my return, but spent most of the late afternoon at a Mess meeting.

Listened to a murder play 'The Night of the Fair' and so to bed. Pleased to receive a Valentine from Joyce today.

151 R.V. (A)
BAFO
Wedy 13.2.47

Dear Dad,

Only a few photos nothing to add to yesterday's letter. Has been snowing heavily here all day and we've had no mail since Monday.

I wonder if you'd be good enough to look out some mal de mer remedy for Joyce and endeavour to pass it to her before she sails? The drug is Hyoscine (sometimes called Scopolamine) Hydrobromide, and my stock is all in 1/100 or 1/150 gm tablets: either will do. You'll find some, I think, in any of these places:
(a) Emergency box
(b) Respirator haversack –
  I think
(c) Sample chest. A little
  cardboard box, containing
  lots of small odd tablet tubes.

This compact (Tiny tube inside another tube)

Friday, 14 February

After taking sick parade, drove down to Lüneburg and saw the second case of mumps we've had.

Back and spent part of the afternoon doing 'Married Families' inoculations. Some book work – this evening read and talked with the staff, as well as writing to Tim who is now at Tel el Kebir.

Bought a small pair of binoculars tonight – 400 cigs, mostly paid in coffee at 4 lb = 100 cigs. So to bed.

Niemeyey Tobacconist, Markplatz. (This shop is still trading today)

Saturday, 15 February

… When the evening came I was able to settle down and develop a couple of films – one, successfully and easily, of my own. Another for a married family, the Venn's, which I did with considerable apprehension, since other people's negatives are something of a trial.

Sunday, 16 February

Took the jeep 'across country' round the perimeter of the drome, to get some aircraft shots, and came back in time to do a couple of Married Family visits.

Whilst in the Mess asked Trudie (*left*), one of our tall, blonde waitresses there, to come up this evening – she looks so terribly lonely and so obviously is miserable and embarrassed at her job.

Immediately after hearing 'Bohème' I was called to see a RAFR man who had had a 'fit'? Meningeal? Epileptic form in the Malcolm Club. When I had got him safely into bed, Trudie arrived and talked to me of her life – she was training as a school teacher in Hamburg during the war.

Monday, 17 February

Up early – fairly ordinary sort of day, slightly marred by rumours from the SMO of a possible impending attachment to some other unit. Am hoping that J will 'freeze' me here by arriving before anything else transpires.

This evening went to the Station Cinema to see 'Pink String and Sealing Wax' … performance further detracted from my having cold feet – and a sense of a developing chill.

Wednesday, 19 February

After tea – and after a day during which I knew every moment meant the chances of J joining me were greater, I got an official notification that she was due to arrive on Friday at 12.26 am.

This evening I had the final letters from Joyce, and one from her father and my own.

Wrote back a letter to Daventry, saw a WAAFI girl with a doubtful salpingitis, then Trudie came round for a cup of tea and offered to provide some flowers for me to give Joyce.

---

151 R.V. (A)
BAFO
20.2.47

Dear Dad,

The big news, of course, is Joyce's impending arrival – she appeared on the strength of BAGO for the first time yesterday, when a signal announced that she will arrive at 12.26 tomorrow, Friday, at Lüneburg. I will, of course, take the ambulance down for her and I hope she will not be held up. If she gets here on the right day, she can meet the squadron at a dinner dance which is being held that evening, as it happens. She and I are staying with some friends here until such time as our home is ready – probably a period of 1–2 wks. I have carefully avoided raising too much fuss over the accommodation problem, lest her passage is postponed – her presence in Germany, is, in the RAF, nine points of the law.

… My pipe is too old to smoke, anyhow. I'm told it is not a Meerschaum but a 'Grandfather's Pipe.' Would look nice, I think, as a stage prop for Faust to smoke in the First Act!

Friday, 21 February

Sick parade as usual, but in a very cheerful and elated mood – then tried to while away the time until 11.50 hrs when I prepared to go down to Lüneburg station to meet J.

Telephone enquiry, then I subsequently discovered that the train would not arrive till 15.00 hrs instead of 12.26, the ship having been held up outside Cuxhaven by ice.

Had lunch in the Mess, collected some pussy willow to greet her and then went down in the ambulance

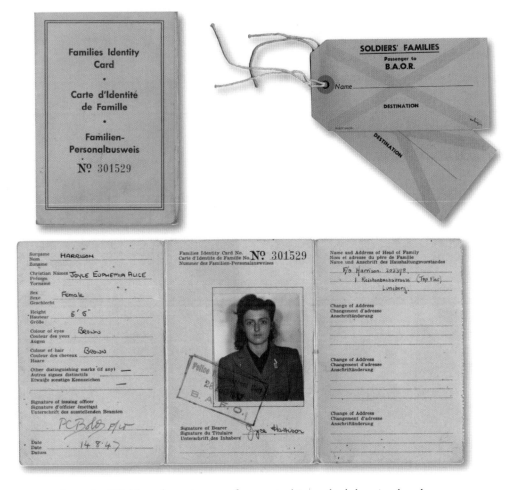

to meet the train. Within a few minutes of my arrival Joyce had detrained and we were on our way back to the Venn's house, where we are to lodge till our flat is ready.

This evening went to a dinner dance at the Mess where J met the rest of the Squadron – all, almost without exception, inebriated. Also introduced her to Trudie. Stayed till just after midnight then back to the house to make the most of two contiguous single beds.

Saturday, 22 February
Only 5 minutes late to take this morning's sick parade, and very little work to do thereafter. Had to go down to the CRS later, so took J down for her first look at Lüneburg, which she saw at a low temperature and through a fairly heavy snow storm.

Officers' Mess, Lüneburg

Sunday, 23 February

Did not rise till 11.45. Then we found everything covered with thick snow. Spent all day indoors, and I wrote some letters and did some work on the books. We had dinner in the house tonight, and then again repaired to SSQ where I bored J – who had to sit in the dark! – by printing last night's films. J rather displeased on the question of whether or not I would continue to do a little flying whilst on this unit.

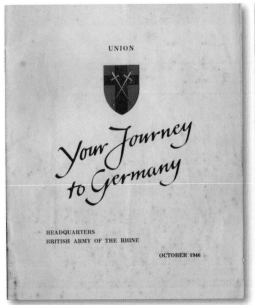

151 R.V. (A)
BAFO
Suny 23.2.47

Dear Dad,

… I eventually met her [Joyce] a couple of minutes before three, looking very well and declaring that she had had a 'wonderful' journey – excellent meals and organization and a comfortable crossing for which no therapy of any form was required.

… It's been snowing steadily since Joyce arrived – today the sun is shining but everywhere is under at least a foot of smooth snow. No mail has come in yesterday or today … Thank you for fixing Joyce up promptly with the (fortunately superfluous) mal de mer tablets. I hope you will find time – there is no hurry at all – to make a sound parcel of my 'Best & Taylor' and send it off. I've 'consumed' an enormous Path. book sent by Ronnie and I am expecting a volume on 'Skins' by the next post. An organized domiciliary existence should improve even existing facilities for some book work.

Yours aye,
Dick

Joyce and the Venns inspecting a German wolfhound out of frame

Tuesday, 25 February

Joyce accompanied me again to Lüneburg this morning and we bought a few cakes and some coffee to take to Trudie tonight. Also our back ration for February – some 1000 cigarettes!

This evening J came down to SSQ – I had just been out to see a 9 wk old baby which its mother had brought to Germany last Friday – not surprising that it now has bronchitis!

18.30 hrs we arrived at Trudie's – she and J seemed to take to each other well and we spent a very pleasant evening talking on Germany and England and exchanging notes on diet, superstitions and customs.

Wednesday, 26 February

Chief event of the day was some flurry about posting – I was detached to Hamburg, but Tonkinson was very reasonable about it when I rang him up, and it seems probable that Thomas will go instead. I like Lüneburg and having T as a friend makes me reluctant to think of leaving it, though it's good to know that Joyce is definitely 'with me'. I hate the transience of service life – I so much like an established home.

This afternoon an airman went crazy and assaulted an S.P. Corporal declaring himself to be the Saviour, and having fits of self depreciation because he wanted to sleep with Paulette Goddard [a 1940's actress briefly married to Chaplin]. We brought him to SSQ, put him to sleep with Nembutal and will send him to Hamburg – presumably a schizophrenic.

151 R.V. (A)
BAFO
Wedy 26.2.47

Dear Dad,

… Joyce is now beginning to get used to Lüneburg – she has had a few strolls round the town, though heavy snow has somewhat hampered her explorations. We went out to spend the evening with a German family I'd met, last night since she – and I – were getting rather 'cheesed' with the restricted conversation of the Service wives here. Tonight we are paying a visit to the Station Cinema.

No professional news – save that I have been called to see an airman who assaulted his colleague and subsequently an S.P. Corporal, on the grounds that they refused to bow down before him 'their Saviour', and were 'Heathens who would not do the will of their Lord God' and interrupted him whilst he was listening to the Divine Mind 'as it revealed itself to him every night between the hours of four and eight.' Quite off his chump, poor chap, and now languishing in Sick Quarters.

Yours aye, Dick

Thursday, 27 February
Down to Lüneburg this morning to buy a few provisions for tonight. This afternoon I went out to see F/Lt Bainbridge's child who has had attacks of vomiting for the past four days. Pretty busy day, with F/O Thomas mostly preoccupied with getting cleared – I am still very pleased, and slightly surprised, that it is not I who am going.

At 18.15 hrs went down to Trudie's by jeep and spent the evening there – which went by very rapidly. Had a light meal with her – some fish off wooden 'plates' – it's very interesting to see how Germans are living today. Stayed there till 22.30 hrs then the usual long walk back – the latter 500 yards in a very cold wind.

So to bed.

A Spitfire in the snow at Lüneburg airfield

German boy with sledge

A slushy Lüneburg street, Kleine Bäckerstraße and Große Bäckerstraße

think you will like

work and, with a warm

MARCH 1947

MARCH 1947

Saturday, 1 March

Up at 08.15 hrs. Fairly busy morning, albeit that part of it was spent down in Lüneburg… This afternoon returned from the Venns' – who are looking after us very kindly but who constantly try to pump me for details of any patients – to SSQ when I spent the afternoon reading and writing.

At 19.15 hrs in a snowstorm that approached at points on the Lüneburg road a blizzard, went down with J in the jeep to collect Trudie and go with her to a revue at the Horrocks Theatre 'Couldn't Care Less'. I bought tickets for this under the impression that a German show was on that night and was correspondingly disappointed.

RH at SSQ

Sunday, 2 March

Did not get up till 10.20 hrs. Went down to SSQ and had a fairly successful session on the bookings, coming back at lunch time only to go back again this afternoon to write to Dad etc. Joyce came down for tea but by the time we had to return she had become irritated by the way in which I had left her on her own all day. So, after I had been out again this evening to print some films, the day finished on a rather sullen note.

Monday, 3 March

Busy day, nothing of major event. Went down to Lüneburg this morning and again this evening – to inspect some binoculars proffered for sale by Schrader, the photographer who has supplied me with several items. He had two nice glasses at 1,200 and 1,000 cigarettes apiece, but I rejected both as a little expensive.

Tuesday, 4 March

Sick parade at 09.00 hrs. Remained in SSQ all morning, pretty busily occupied with release medicals etc. Rather quieter this afternoon, so I was able to gave a good couple of hours on the books.

Thursday, 6 March

One of the heaviest sick parades (25) to date this morning, followed by a batch of releases so that I begin to feel I am earning my salary for once.

… More 'medicals' this afternoon with one of the minor operations (removal of a facial wart) which now form the highlights of my surgical practice – I am speedily reaching the stage when I myself cannot believe I once opened abdomens, performed mastectomies etc. I try to make up by reading furiously …

When we came to leave SSQ on our way back to the Venns, we found the road down literally a sheet of ice, with a stranded 15cwt lorry slipping about helplessly on it.

Sunday, 9 March

I was hoping for a quiet morning to myself for some revision and letters, but it appeared essential that I should go to a cocktail meeting, or sherry party, or what you will at the C.O.'s house. So I went along, much against my will and sat there being 'bound rigid' from 11.45 hrs – 13.00 hrs: came back and finished the morning with Joyce in a very bad grace.

In the afternoon – it was bright and sunny, and the standing snow was beginning to thaw off – the Venns, Joyce and I walked down to inspect progress at our flat. This time Mrs Venn's conversation drove me into a bad temper.

Joyce and our hostess going to Sunday morning sherry with the CO

Joyce watching a German child playing in the snow

ON ACTIVE SERVICE
LETTER FORM

151 Rua   6.3.47
BAFO
BAOR

Dear Dad,

Our flat is rendered more habitable every day now and it seems pretty definite
that we will take up residence on Saturday or Monday next. The long delay
is due to the fact that all the radiators were burst by frost, and that the flat
generally was in a pretty poor state of repair. Whether I will spend all my life
in Lüneburg then, I do not know – it may prove unsatisfactory to be so far
from SSQ and the airfield. On the other hand, the 'Married Quarters' on the
camp, occupied by a bunch of over-fed under worked officers' wives with all the
resultant chat, has already come near to driving Joyce and I 'nutty!'

I'm feeling the pinch now Thomas has gone and am pretty hard worked all day
– wouldn't be so bad if such a lot of time wasn't taken up, not by any clinical
work, but by doing routine examinations or writing official reports.

…Alice would be interested in a purchase I made the other day, via someone
'in the know' at a German gramophone factory at Hannover – 32 discs,
brand new, at a cost approximately to 7d each, all 'highbrow' – Peer Gynt,
Siegfried, Tosca, Tristan & Isolde, Chopin, Schubert, Bartered Bride, Thieving
Magpie, Merry Wives of Windsor, etc. etc. I hope she will be able to hear them
eventually.

Yours aye,

Dick

Monday, 10 March

Another sunny day, with the roads clearing fast. This morning Joyce took occupation of our new residence – the flat, with 3 rooms, plus kitchen and bathroom, at the top of Reichenbachstraße 1.

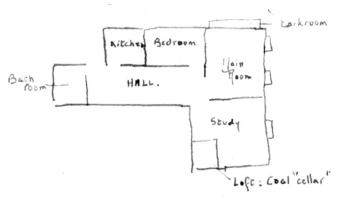

I had a big sick parade, and spent a hectic morning phoning round, 'laying on' the necessary facilities. At lunch time I went down to Lüneburg (to buy a compass for myself, incidentally) and to pick J up for lunch at the Venns'. She went back to the chaos of unpacked furniture, painters and electricians after the meal and I joined her when my work was finished. Arrived to find Trudie with her, rendering yeoman service.

Joyce and RH in their newly acquired flat

View from the flat window

Tuesday, 11 March

Awoke to find it had snowed heavily overnight, and to sample some of the joys of rising in an unheated house with the cooking facilities still u/s. Joyce correspondingly despondent…. I went off to SSQ, leaving her to the chaos of piled up furniture and the mercies of the painters and Dienstgruppe…. Trudie again assisting us – we sat round our boiler and talked … it had stopped snowing by now, but all over the streets are thick drifts.

Wednesday, 12 March

Everything a bit better this morning – fire going, kitchen warm and even hot water. Pleasanter day in SSQ, so that I even found time to write a couple of letters.

Had a bath and then 'home' to the flat – our last 'untidy' night as I hope. Trudie came round about 19.45 hrs for a meal. Then we talked – round the kitchen stove this time – and, after seeing Trudie off, retired to bed.

Dear Dad   12.3.47

Only a brief note (a) because I'm feeling the effects of working on my own at a
busy time of year and (b) because I'm very fully occupied with my move into the
new flat.... As you can imagine, everything is still a bit of a chaos – Joyce reigns
amidst a pile of furniture over eight or nine P.O.W.s, some of whom are still
putting the finishing touches on the paintwork. I think though, that things should
be straightening themselves out tomorrow, and we should be quite tidy by the
week end.

Yours aye,
Dick

Photography, of course, suspended for this week – more 'pictures' as soon as I'm
settled in.

Main room with RH's microscope at 1 Reichenbachstraße

Thursday, 13 March
Awoken at 05.45 hrs by vigorous knocking at the door – a driver to tell me of a call to a F/Sgt's wife who had gone into labour prematurely. Dressed and went down to her flat, subsequently transporting her to the cold, inefficient CRS in the town, when I left her as soon as I decently could, and returned for an hour more in bed.

To SSQ only five minutes later than usual – fortunately a quiet morning's work. I was able to go down to the CRS at 11.30 hrs to see how my patient was faring – and arrived just after she had been delivered by an Army Dr, after a very short second-stage.

Friday, 14 March
Ambulance broke down this morning so I had to walk to SSQ – in the deep puddles and roads full of the slush consequent upon a rapid thaw which set in early today. Started late on a big sick parade and subsequently had to go out twice to see a W/O's wife suffering from a puzzling combination of diarrhoea and apparently excruciating back ache – a syndrome in which I could only assume there was a large cortical element and for which I could not administer anything more specific than a dose of morphine.

Saturday, 15 March
A fairly quiet morning – which, I had hoped would preface an afternoon 'off duty' down in Lüneburg. Alas! Mrs S, the miscarriage of earlier in the week, had to be transported to Hamburg and – since there was a definite possibility of her going into labour en route – I felt bound to accompany her. J – rather disgruntled at this disruption of our plans – came along too. The trip was, however, uneventful. And – since we were not long in Hamburg, and since all the shops were closed – was unprofitable. Rather 'dicey' drive back in the dark over a freezing road; returned to flat at 20.30 hrs.

Sunday, 16 March
… stayed indoors for the rest of the evening save for a brief visit I had to pay to SSQ to see a # [medical notation for a fracture] lacrimal bone and to reduce under chloroform, a dislocated shoulder in a man with a history of three previous similar dislocations.

Bomb damage evident in Hamburg

Tuesday, 18 March

Still rather wet underfoot – river rising steadily here, but nowhere near a danger level. Tonight's news, however, gives details of record floods in the Severn and Thames valleys.

Trudie spent the day and evening with Joyce – proceedings ending on rather a quiet note when T expressed emphatic disapproval of a BBC German talk about – as far as I could gather – the last days of the Hitler regime. (This, of course, leaving me unmoved but arousing Joyce who saw Trudie off, after apparently a very pleasant day, rather sullenly.)

Back home after taking Trudie to hers to consume the 'News of the World' together and to discussing the case of Mrs C and her masochist late husband.

Wednesday, 19 March

Busy all morning, but this afternoon made an abortive trip into Lüneburg in search of various photographic accessories. After writing to Dad, returned to the flat via Mr

RH's jeep during the floods

Schrader's room where I negotiated for the purchase of a very lovely microscope.

After working for an hour, and having dinner, J and I went to the cinema next door to us and saw 'The Killers' – an elaboration of Ernest Hemmingway's story about a man hunted down and killed for a previous 'double-cross'.

Dear Dad   *19.3.47*

Have been following with interest the wireless and Press reports of the flood crisis in the U.K.… BAFO doesn't seem at all a bad place in comparison with the U.K. just now … though Lüneburg is pretty slushy, with some roads submerged, and we experienced the big storm of Sunday a few hours after you. Joyce and I are snugly dug in now and beginning to feel quite at home.… Joyce had a chance of a look at Hamburg, after which we returned.

Thursday, 20 March

Up early for quite a busy day – the ambulance went out 3 times. Once for a German, run over by a petrol bowser and severely shocked … a second time for a RAF bod hit by a piece of metal: and again for an S.P. taken suddenly ill with a condition I presume to be food poisoning.

Also had several married families to visit; one child, abt 1½ yrs. I sent to Hamburg – she had a severe chickenpox with well mkd. toxaemia and secondary infection; oedema of the lids completely closing her eyes.

This evening Trudie and her mother came to dinner – everyone very annoyed because the Smiths walked into the end of our evening together. Bought a very fine microscope tonight, and this morning was very pleased to receive three fine instruments … from our driver Paddy who bought them yesterday in Hamburg.

Friday, 21 March

Much quieter day today – several 'families visits' but nothing spectacular. Temperature warmer, and the roads at last really clear of snow.

This evening, after doing an hour's work, went out to Monica Hein's house – she had been an object of interest in the past to some press photographer – and took away a photo flood for 300 cigs – she wants to buy a pair of shoes.

Saturday, 22 March

Very leisurely morning, and for the first time could enjoy having the windows open during sick parade. Finished at 12.15 hrs and came home to lunch – found Trudie there, for she had called to tell J of a new job she had found at the Lüneburg telephone exchange.

This afternoon J and I went out into Lüneburg and had cream cakes for tea at the Y.M.C.A. Home, and then out to the Horrock's Theatre to see 'Room for Two', one of those true-to-type over farcical farces with which I am fast becoming familiar.

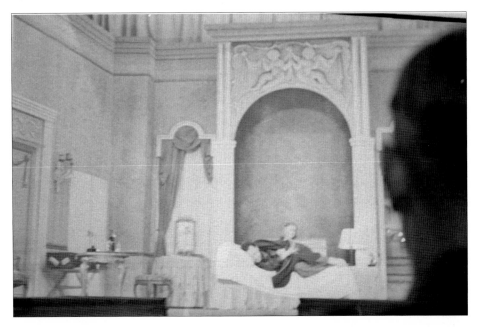

Horrock's Theatre, 'Room for Two'

Watching inspection from SSQ

Sunday, 23 March

Did not get up until 10.30 hrs. But during the day I managed to get in well over two hours' work on the books, to take some photos, develop a film and do the prints from another.

We went out for a walk this afternoon, but a threatening sky made us turn back and we arrived home just in time to avoid a downpour.

Had to go out this evening to see F/L W, taken ill with vomiting and abdominal pains. Failed to convince myself that he had appendicitis and, a little dubiously, admitted him to SSQ and returned to the flat.

Dear Dad   *23.3.47*

Incidentally I've obtained a very good – albeit not brand new – microscope this week. Quadruple nosepiece – two different oil immersion objectives, four oculars, mechanical stage, focusing subtage condenser with interchangeable oil immersion dark ground condenser. I consider it a very good bargain at £7/10/'s worth of the local 'currency' accumulated over a long period. But I'll probably need that 'small overdraft' when it comes to passing the Customs on my return!

I've applied for Continental leave for 14 days from May 7th next – I would like to return home to see you all, but I'm afraid that the cost of Joyce's passage would be prohibitive: apart from which I believe one's consort may not be able to return again until a passage is available. Again, it does seem a little foolish when we have a chance to see something new to spend a leave back in the UK – particularly under circumstances such as prevail there now! Do you realise that our butter ration for one week is equivalent to yours for three? Perhaps we can find a way of sending some grub later – (at present we give it away to odd Germans!) So we are trying to arrange accommodation, via Alec, at a resort in the Hartz mountains on the edge of the Britischë Zone … things are very indefinite at the moment.

Monday. 24 March

Rose at 08.07 hrs – a quiet enough day for me to come down to Lüneburg on some photographic shopping this morning and to take a driving test with F/O Noble this afternoon.

W still a bit of a problem – pain much less prominent now, but has vomited 2x today and is running a high temperature and looks rather ill.

My ambulance driver bought back a very nice Dial pattern sphygmanometer and a useful drill and bits tonight from Hamburg – I am looking forward to making a trip myself into the city later this week.

Tuesday, 25 March

Hefty sick parade this morning, but I failed to detect any malingerers. This afternoon I took the jeep round the perimeter track for a few snaps of the aircraft 'graveyard' at the far end of the aerodrome.

Aircraft graveyard, Lüneburg (He2190wl)

Finally decided to send F/L W into Hamburg this evening, wondering yet whether I have been 'sitting on' an appendicitis all this time and still very puzzled.

Monica Hein left SSQ today – rather to my regret. The Sgt. has triumphed! He has been trying to get rid of her for a long time now.

Wednesday, 26 March

'The M.O.'s day out': up at 07.15 hrs and took sick parade at 08.30 hrs. Finished at 09.20 hrs and left for Hamburg in the ambulance, with very fine weather. En route took some pictures of the Autobahn. On arrival at 94th General Hospital, however, the day was marred by my hearing that W was on the 'D.I.' [dangerously ill] list with a perforated appendix and generalized peritonitis – a retro-iliac appendix, which I should have suspected earlier, though I still think, retrospectively, it could not have been certainly diagnosed.

Then to the centre of Hamburg, where I visited three surgical instrument shops in rapid succession, buying some good tools but getting 'on the track' of some even better ones.

Did not have any lunch – consumed four cream cakes and two cups of tea in a Church Army canteen, then went in search of a tripod and ordered a flash bulb apparatus and some filters. Left Hamburg at 16.20 hrs … had a slight headache on arrival and after dinner did nothing more energetic than sitting down to read *The Lancet*.

Thursday, 27 March

Up at 06.00 hrs to see J off. T called for her, and they went up to Hamburg with the latter's mother for the day. Quiet and uneventful time in SSQ with nothing remarkable – no appreciable change, as I learnt on the phone, in W's condition.

Home this evening and lit the wire and did some book work whilst awaiting J's return – the party came back at about 21.30 hrs. J had an interesting day, meeting some friends of T's in Hamburg, but this meeting plus fairly continuous light rain, had prevented her visiting any of the shops … Had to see a child … with some mental retardment this morning after it had had an epileptic fit.

Friday, 28 March

Quiet day – this afternoon S/L Sewell took me up for my first flight in a Mosquito – when we did a circuit before coming in at 300 mph. I thought it was going to be my last! Took some – probably indifferent – photographs through the perspex.

HE219 (Owl)

Dear Dad   *30.3.47*

Weather quite warm and fine recently – I had a 'day off' this week and I went up to Hamburg for a stroll round and bought a few more tools etc. some of which I will send but the best of which I retain here. Flying has started again too, and I've had my christening on a Mosquito, with a few 'shoot-ups' showing a modest 350 on the clock. But I chose the O.C. Flying, who was Wavell's personal pilot, to take me up!

My 'jeep' has gone u/s for some obscure reason, so I've been given a 15 cwt for this weekend. In future I'll be able to talk to Subaltern Harrison on his own ground!

Yours, aye, Dick

Saturday, 29 March

Finished off a quiet morning by having my hair cut and taking out a 15 cwt truck, lent to me in place of my jeep. Home for dinner, with Tim's first letter from Jerusalem – giving, however, very little detail of his activities.... This afternoon we went for a short stroll in Lüneburg and had our customary cream cakes for tea in the YMCA.

Tea and cream cakes at the YMCA (note the logo on the cup)

Sunday, 30 March

Up at 10.30 hrs, but very little work this morning, for I had to pay a routine visit to SSQ – again driving with considerable difficulty, this 15 cwt truck. And no sooner had I returned home than I had to go down again for a minor suture job.

J very depressed and in tears after lunch – feeling, I gather, the loneliness and intellectual isolation of her position in Lüneburg. However, she soon cheered up and tonight we went down to the Horrock's Theatre for a Continental variety show – a very good one by English standards, but poor in comparison with that I saw with S/L Sewell earlier in the year. Home, coffee and bed.

Monday, 31 March

Lengthy sick parade this morning, but after that nothing at all – was able to go down to Lüneburg and then buy some flash powder – and an exposure meter subsequently retailed to a colleague for 50 cigs. profit!

A Churchill ARV Mark II, these were based on Churchill III or IV tanks with their turrets removed and replaced with a dummy turret and gun.

Churchill tank, Cavalry barracks, Lüneburg

Meanwhile

think you will like

work and, with a

warm

R

Desi

APRIL 1947

APRIL 1947

Tuesday, 1 April

… Very pleased to receive, via one of my drivers, a handsome Oculus opthalmoscope and a pair of double action bone nibblers, both ordered when I visited Hamburg.

This afternoon did a 'sanitary round' of the cookhouse, bringing back with me a piece of pork for our supper. Home to listen to 'Appointment with Fear', to develop another under-exposed film, have a read and so to bed.

Wednesday, 2 April

Probably my quietest day yet on 151 RU(A) … because of odd interruptions I have rather given up serious work during the day, on my books – I rather wasted the time pottering round. Reluctant to do another sanitary round or display any great administrative zeal, for the labour seems to bring neither intellectual profit nor – such is the way of a service which may suddenly post me elsewhere tomorrow or in six months time – official advancement.

'The Third Man' played at the Horrocks Theatre by Marius Goring and Lucie Mankheim – it was a very real pleasure to see good acting in a straight play after the usual run of usual 'actors' in the usual farces. Really a very refreshing evening.

Thursday, 3 April

Fairly quiet in SSQ – went down to Lüneburg during the morning and this afternoon took the jeep for a run round the 'drome, taking a few snaps en route. Found half a dozen

live cannon shells in the aircraft 'graveyard' and brought them back to the armourer.

Joyce came down to SSQ at 16.20 hrs and I gave her – and myself – a 'typhus vaccine inj'. In consequence of which I felt a little 'off' during the evening and spent it very quietly reading.

RH Jeep and Churchill tank

Dear Dad   *Wedy 2.4.47*

Joyce and I are still quite well – any indigestion experienced is the result of overfeeding, I think – we have to give away great chunks of meat every other day and when summer comes it will be a problem to eat butter fast enough. We have so much bacon that Joyce now makes it into meat pies. I haven't used any saccharine since I saw the white cliffs at Bexhill disappear. There are only two snags – one, milk – fresh milk is forbidden on sanitary grounds, and the supply of tins is restricted. Two – potatoes… until recently we were using only the dehydrated variety. Supplies of fresh fruit, too, are rather intermittent though we get an abundance of the dried variety with a couple of tins of pears and peaches each week. Re emergencies – our flat is on the 'phone: I have no 'stabling' facilities, so a jeep or ambulance is sent down for me when required, and to pick me up every morning. As for your post-war car – I nearly bought you a Jeep for £20 in France, but the petrol consumption is heavy and spares will soon be in short supply. They are not, anyhow, the ideal family car and I can't see myself driving one in a fashionable practice. Would a Volkswagen do?

Friday, 4 April

Did not rise until 10.00 hrs and at 11.00 hrs went down to SSQ just to check out a few cases. Also visited a child I saw ill yesterday and on whom I failed to make any diagnosis – today it had obvious chickenpox.

Saturday, 5 April

Grey morning, becoming brighter in the afternoon – spent the forenoon down in SSQ taking a short sick parade and examining a 'PUO' – ill for about four days with pyrexia malaise etc. and today showing a pink blotchy macular eruption on the trunk. I submitted the case to the 94th as one of 'Enteric' – since he had no occipital lymphadenopathy and he believed he had previously had rubella. However, I am told the eventual diagnosis in Hamburg was, nevertheless, 'German measles'.

Trudie came to lunch – afterwards we ascended the 'Kalkberg' on the periphery of the city, and I found it an ideal spot from which to take some snaps. Tea at the YMCA.

RH admiring the view of Lüneburg from Kalkberg, the cap rock of a salt dome
in the western part of the town.

Trudie and Joyce on Kalkberg

Sunday, 6 April

Gale blowing all night, and intermittent, and often heavy, rain all day. I rose early to attend Communion but missed the service, as we subsequently discovered, because we did not know that the clocks had been advanced overnight!

Most of day indoors, but had a short run down to SSQ and returned to partake of an ingenious 'Easter Cake' made by Joyce.

At 20.00 hrs we went to a 'Continental' Variety show at the Horrock's Theatre – good seats at the middle of front row and some excellent turns – Marionettes, a very

 versatile musician (12 instruments) and much ballet – but J a little unnerved by a man almost directly over us swaying on a springy steel pole and a trapeze artist similarly situated!

Gave J a work basket for an Easter present and received a blotter from her.

Monday, 7 April

… Quiet evening at Trudie's thereafter – I forgot a book I intended reading there, I got slightly bored. Joyce spent a couple of hours untangling a lot of silk and got slightly irritable. When we returned home I spent about 1½ hours printing the films taken on Saturday last and felt extremely gratified at the results.

Tuesday, 8 April

Lengthy sick parade today, as I anticipated. The rest of the day though, I spent at the RAF regiment assault course, watching a lot of Phosphorus bombs and Ammonal and coarse invective directed against the unfortunates scaling the obstacles there, and taking about a dozen snaps.

Home for an evening's work, reading and listening to the wireless – but had to go out in the pouring rain to see a child with bronchitis …

RAF Regiment Assault Course

Wednesday, 9 April

Rainy sort of day and nothing really interesting to note – evening on the books and developed a film strip – disappointed about some shots being spoilt by air bubbles sticking to the film.

Dear Dad   *Wedy 9.4.47*

Pleased to know that my receiver has arrived, and sorry to see you speaking so slightingly of it. It's really a very fine job – an eleven valve communications receiver, all the valves interchangeable. If you undo two small studs on the front with a screwdriver or a penny (push, then turn) you will be able to admire the beautiful way in which it is built and the perfection of the wave-band change mechanism with its revolving bezel. Even after defraying the railway costs from the aerodrome I consider it a bargain for my '50 Free Issue'!

Nothing fresh from this part of the globe – weather indifferent for the most part, but we had a fine day yesterday. Some colonel visited the RAF Regt. here, who put on an Assault Course demonstration with 'live' Brens and bags of Phosphorus and Gun cotton, so I had to be in evidence. I toddled round (minus pack or rifle of course!) as well, so I hope to have some good pictures to show … Bags of casualties, but nothing spectacular – only sprains etc.

Thursday, 10 April

Ordinary sick parade and release examination this morning – kept fairly busy in SSQ all morning. This afternoon, more routine jobs and another shot at the tissue resection operation for an ingrowing toenail.

Very pleased to have some of Tim's letters and snaps from Dad – his doings in Jerusalem sound very interesting but there is little doubt that he would like to get back to the Mauritius job – the difference is probably like that between my position here and in the Rhône valley.

Friday, 11 April

Set off in the ambulance and picked up J – she's *never* quite ready – and proceeded to Hamburg, me riding in the back with the usual crew of syphilitics and F/O N, the young gentleman who always looks so much like the type who is 'drinking himself to death' – only this time it was scabies for which he was consulting the profession. Arrived at 94th BMH at about 10.45 and I popped in to see W, who looked very pale and has obviously lost a bit of flesh but is, nevertheless, out of danger now.

Afterwards J and I ran round the shops – they shut at 15.00 hrs and we had to manage some lunch at this famous Atlantic Hotel on the shore of the Alster before then. Actually we did quite a lot of purchasing – J buying the simple little vases and trinkets which always appeal to her so much, whilst I collected the usual surgical instruments at the usual ludicrous prices. I felt ashamed to plonk down ten cigarettes as payment for half a dozen useful tools and had to add some chocolate as well ... Lunch in this sumptuous hotel resolved itself into pilchards, pigs heart and semolina, but we enjoyed it ... It was

Hamburg Reesendammbrücke and the Kleine Alster

pleasant, sitting in the 'Atlantic' with all its nautical frescoes. Hamburg actually is quite a seafaring place – every other shop has its little galleon in the windows – and I reflect with professional wistfulness on the wealth of rare pathological material that must pass through its hospitals – there is at least one devoted to tropical diseases.

Saturday, 12 April
Usual morning in SSQ – uneventful and undisturbed afternoon, at the end of which we went to the cinema next door to see the film – we have *heard* it twice nightly for several days – 'My Darling Clementine' a modern old time Western. So back to hear 'Passing of the 3rd floor back' and to bed.

Joyce looking out of the top floor flat on Reichenbachstraße

Sunday, 13 April
J and I went for a walk along the Winsen road for about an hour this afternoon, then returned to listen to an adaptation of the 1918 escape story 'Road to Endor'.

Monday, 14 April

Busy but uneventful day – had the first of the anticipated 'stir-up' calls from the CO who is worried about my apparent neglect of sanitary administration – for which, with all the 'clinical' duties to attend to single handed, I now have little time.

Lectures today and tomorrow to some senior NCOs on 'Hygiene' – during which I mostly talk about VD because I know more about that!

Tuesday, 15 April

The most interesting event of the day was an Anson's crash landing this morning – was called down to the tarmac at 11.30 and the machine – from Bückeburg – circled overhead soon after, with its undercarriage stuck up. Hung about on the tarmac whilst rockets were fired to enable the machine to find the 'drome, and I took some pictures of the crash party standing by. About 12.35 it eventually came in, making a very long run and bumping slightly. Both airscrews were feathered horizontally – the idea of the CO, who superintended the 'talking-in' – and the only damage was a bent pitot-head! Still, the waiting period was all very exciting and my first experience of such an event.

Smoke Indicator Rockets at Lüneburg airfield

The Crash Team waiting for the Anson to land

The Anson after it landed safely (markings show it to have been used by a Three Star General of the British Army of the Rhine)

Dear Dad   *Wedy 16.4.47*

We had our first crash call yesterday – an Anson on test from Bückburg got lost in a bit of low cloud about lunch time, and couldn't get its undercarriage down.
It was directed to this 'drome and the poor blighter flew up and down the tarmac, looking at the fire tender and ambulance and trying to use up petrol whilst Flying Control 'talked it in'. Eventually, after about three-quarters of an hour of this he came in – ambulance, tender and my jeep running down the 'drome with him. He bumped up and down a bit and looked like sticking his nose in at one point, but finished up very nicely, with the plane only slightly damaged and the crew only a little 'shook'. You may get some interesting snaps when I develop my present spool.

Wednesday, 16 April

Another warm, sunny day, and a fairly quiet one in SSQ. I went out to inspect the dope shop this morning and this afternoon spent a few minutes at a demonstration on the Assault course. Got back to the flat early, but found all the neighbours' children in possession being entertained to tea by J who seems to work off a lot of her maternal instincts in this way.

Thursday, 17 April
Uneventful morning, but a bombshell at lunch, when S/L Purdie told me he had received a signal from AM to say I had not the right to Married Quarters – a matter which, apparently, has only just come to light!

This threat to J's continued stay over here rather clouded the otherwise amusing 'Fly Control' Conference held this afternoon at the OC's instigation, when he proposed the most whole-hearted measures for dealing with the problem – at times suggesting that we were in the Panama Canal Zone instead of a non-malarial area of Europe. Anyhow, I put my little piece over without revealing much of my ignorance as regards matters hygienic and then afterwards sounded him about my own problem – he seemed willing to take the 'play for time' attitude which, I think, affords every prospect of success for us.

Another view of the flat on Reichenbachstraße

Friday, 18 April

… Joyce and I went down to SSQ and thence to the Mess for a so-called 'Social Evening for the Married Families'. This consisted of a gathering of half a dozen couples playing Housey-Housey and Horse Racing in a half-hearted fashion under the eye of the G/I who was principally responsible for promoting the whole function. It was interesting to see S/L Marquis, the RC padre, quite definitely inebriated and talking rubbish. Otherwise the evening was a 'dead loss'.

Saturday, 19 April

I decided to take the day 'off' as regards my revision and after dinner at the flat went back to the unit and spent the afternoon in the sunlight on the 'drome, watching the activities of the gliding club which I have joined. Cross winds prevented the use of the Primary Trainer – a flying birdcage creation of string and fabric which looks very frail indeed. My own participation got no further than taking a series of photographs for when the wind finally subsided and I was strapped in the trainer, the cable broke and it came on to rain. I returned home and spent the evening reading after developing a film.

The Primary Trainer – 'a flying birdcage made of string and fabric' [German SG38 Schulgleiter]

The gliding club in action

Kranich glider

Sunday, 20 April

… Immediately after dinner out to the 'drome, full of gliding zeal. I did a good 'groundslide' without any snags though a little frightened at the unexpectedly high speeds attained. About half an hour later, quite confidently, I essayed a 'low hop'. The CO arrived as I strapped myself in and cracked the usual jest about my being the only doctor available … many a true word in jest! I tore across the 'drome and found myself 20–30 ft in the air before I knew where I was. I jettisoned the cable and came down very fast, hitting the ground with quite a bump and soaring off again. Again I pulled the stick back, but this time the plane didn't change its trim and I came down on the nose and one wing, an almighty bump. I saw my glasses get jogged off and then picked myself out of the seat and felt for a compression fracture – none there fortunately. But the mainspar of the wing had snapped, many joints were strained – and my behind has punched a hole in the plywood seat. Soon after I had a lift in the dual control Kranich, but I felt very nervous and tonight I seriously wonder whether I shall ever have the courage to sit on the end of the wire again!

F.L. Venn being strapped into the cockpit of a Grunau glider by Ziggy the instructor

Monday, 21 April
This evening got back to the flat fairly early and had a good two hours' work on the books. Was very cheered when my driver returned from Hamburg bringing back the slides mentioned in my entry of the 11th last. A beautifully prepared set of about 360 pathological specimens, many of them somewhat of a rarity … They form a beautiful group for revision or teaching purposes and constitute a fine acquisition for 720 RM – representing the conversion of a week's ration of 130 cigarettes (about 7/6d).

Tuesday, 22 April
Uneventful morning – this afternoon made a reconnaissance of the pond behind the aerodrome that I am charged with oiling. Home fairly early and put in an hour on the books before going down to the library to change my novel. Then had to go back to the 'drome for a crash landing scare that turned out to be a false alarm.

Wednesday, 23 April
Put in a couple of good hours on the books this evening and was getting my gear out for some photographic printing when the town fire siren sounded. Looked out and saw a promising blaze and put my coat on to see what it was all about – quite a small shed, very well alight and fanned by a strong wind. Soon got tired of watching though, and came home and carried on with my printing.

Thursday, 24 April
Another pretty dull day, another good night of revision and finished up with an hour on my slides and new microscope. So to bed.

Friday, 25 April
This afternoon, taking advantage of a warm day, I inflated a bomber dinghy, borrowed from the Safety Section and, mounting it on top of a jeep, took it down to a pond on the airfield perimeter. There, with the assistance of three members of SSQ staff, set about covering the surface of the water with old fuel oil – a very greasy performance.

The bomber dinghy strapped to the roof of the jeep

The dinghy afloat

Mosquito spraying

Dear Dad   *Saty 26.4.47*

We have had a very pleasant mild spell recently, and the flies and mosquitoes are now beginning to put in an appearance to mar things somewhat. Still, I had a half day's 'holiday' last week when I took some of my gallant men down to the local pond and sailed a Bomber dinghy over it for a couple of hours under the pretence of putting down an oil layer on the water to kill the insect larvae. (Photos, no doubt, will follow.)

A few more maps enclosed for the family collection herewith …

We are looking forward to our 'first leave' but feel rather perturbed about it — the booking of our hotel has been left to Joyce's brother, who first put us onto the place, and at the moment we are awaiting some confirmation of his having fixed us up. Goodness knows where we will go at short notice if the Hahnenklee project falls through.

Saturday, 26 April
Quiet morning – this afternoon J and I went out for a stroll round the town … and concluded it, as usual, with cream cakes at the YMCA. Evening indoors reading, but also did about 3 hrs revision today … and, now that I am beginning to buckle down to Anatomy and Physiology, Primary FRCS no longer seems quite as impossible as once it did … but still difficult enough.

Sunday, 27 April
Find myself quite attached to the old flat now, and I view with aversion any proposal that I should move back to the 'drome. Though unfortunately, if what I hear is correct, the G/C may demand such a move when accommodation becomes available.

Joyce writing in the flat at Reichenbachstraße

Monday, 28 April
For a Monday, a surprisingly quiet day, though quite a bunch of expectant mothers came up for their periodic overhaul this afternoon … Joyce and I went to 'Great Expectations' when John Mills and the dramatic depictions of Jaggers and the Old Convict, held us enthralled through a long story till 22.30 hrs.

Tuesday, 29 April

Today was given up to the SMO's visit – he (S/L Tonkinson) arrived at about 11.30 hrs, with his wife, who was bundled off to Joyce's care during the rest of the day, whilst 'Tonk' energetically inspected SSQ, dismissed the supply and demand of MOs with the G/C and checked this year's DDs – quite in error – against last year's register.

He left at 15.00 hrs, inviting J and I to a weekend at his house, whilst I returned to the unit to give a lecture on hygiene and to collect a Voightlander Bessa which I won in the Station draw, for J.

Wednesday, 30 April

Home early and – having taken advantage of the quiet evening at Trudie's to write my mid-week letter home – I had a good session with a book on the Special Air Service 'Born of the Desert' lent to me by A/S Sewall.

This afternoon I was able to go down to Lüneburg and was pleased to find a few new instruments (Volkmann's spoon, Adenoid curette etc.) in the surgical shop. En route back to the Camp was stopped to give some first aid to a German woman who had had her fingertip crushed in a minor smash with a 15 cwt. Gave her a slightly superfluous 1/2 gm Omnopon [morphia] from a Tubunic and sent her on to the hospital.

Old houses in Lüneburg, subsiding due to salt mining

Meanwh[ile]

think you will like

work and, with a warm

R
Dex

MAY 1947

MAY 1947

Thursday, 1 May

Wet day, and the lull in SSQ activities continues. Used it to have a bath and came home to put in about 2–3 hours on revision before settling down to another reading session. We are planning to have a 'leave' next week, and when we return I think I will start my old pre-qualification habit of early rising on summer mornings to do some work before breakfast.

Friday, 2 May

Stayed in, reading and working, this evening.

Saturday, 3 May

Quiet morning – usual stroll round the shops and 'cream cake' tea this afternoon. Read, worked and wrote letters this evening. So to bed.

Sunday, 4 May

A very full day – rose at 10.15 hrs and did a little work before an early lunch, being interrupted only by a couple of 'special sick', brought down to my flat to receive attention. And by Cpl. Cordon coming into say his goodbyes.

Had an early lunch, and got round to the YMCA before 14.00 hrs to board a bus going on a 'liberty run' to Hagenbeck's Tiergarten [Zoo] at Hamburg. Arrived there about 15.40 hrs and spent 1 hr 20 mins wandering round the animals. There was a bigger collection than I had expected – bears, camels, seals etc. all grouped compactly in a beautifully designed park – an improvement in its arrangement to our own zoo, though the number of animals can never have been so great. All looked very hungry and very appreciative of any food tendered by visitors. I took some photographs and even gained entrance (1 cig.) to the lions' cage.

Home after a tea at the Hamburg YMCA at 19.30 hrs. Out again almost immediately with Joyce to a performance at St Michaelkirche of a Beethoven symphony (9th).

Monday, 5 May

Rose at 07.30 hrs and went down to SSQ for a rather full sick parade, which I dealt with as quickly as I could. Left with the ambulance, picking up J en route and arrived at the 94th BMH at 11.30 hrs approx. Paid a fleeting visit to W – and to Barclay, convalescent after an operation for a polyp and a Caldwell Luc – partly out of courtesy and partly to justify my trip officially. Then J and I set out on a tour of the shops in the Ganse Markt and Jungefend Str. – my most notable acquisition being a pair of ring-form biopsy forceps such as I have been trying to obtain for some time.

Lunch in the Atlantic, which we enjoyed as usual, and then some more shopping – we bought a small galleon on a wall bracket, something I have always wanted.

… J and I spent the evening with J at Monica Heine's house, principally discussing her opinions of the Jewish problem and of the Hitler régime.

Tuesday, 6 May

… rather slack working day, for X seemed disinclined to exert himself to the extent of taking over any earlier than was absolutely essential.

This evening J and I went to the cinema to see *Green For Danger* – an English film of a murder mystery with some very authentic hospital scenes as a background. We both enjoyed it very much – J being thrilled by the suspense and I by some of the finer touches of detail, like the correct pre-opping of a head surgery case. Not quite so sure that an alert anaesthetist wouldn't notice that he was poisoning a patient with CO_2 if the cylinders were wrongly painted. Perhaps big doses would cause a rapid collapse without many premonitory signs?

Wednesday, 7 May

My first day of leave, so rose late and had a stroll round Lüneburg to make a few purchases. Then, after lunch, went back to the airfield to pack away some luggage, collect travelling warrants etc. preparatory to our departure tomorrow. I spent the evening reading and then printing some of my films. So to bed.

F/O X, it seems, took advantage of his first day on duty to go off in the ambulance to Hamburg!

Thursday, 8 May

The day of our departure – up at about 09.00 hrs, and Joyce exceedingly irritable and bad tempered until, after a very hot walk down to the station, where our arrival just coincided with that of the train, we finally got under way at 11.35 hrs.

Travelled in comfort to Hannover, where we arrived about 14.15 hrs and retired to the stuffy Nissen hut that houses the Red Shield Club to eat our sandwiches plus some tea and a couple of cakes.

German civilian train – with a British coach having bare wooden seats – at 16.38 hrs and travelled via Hildesheim and a host of very small stations until about 19.40 hrs. At that time – after gradually noticing an increasing hilliness of the country – arrived at Goslar, a pretty little open town. But found, of course, no transport to meet us despite my previous phone calls. Travelled up steep pine-walled roads to Hahnenklee, 15 km away, and wandered round for some time with our weighty bags looking for the Anzio Club (*see below*), at which we are to stay. Found it at last, changed and had dinner …

Anzio Officer's Club
Goslar

Dear Dad   *Fri 9.5.47*

*Just to let you know that our holiday is underway at last – having evacuated
all our more important possessions from the flat to SSQ for the duration of our
absence. We left Lüneburg yesterday morning and took train to Hannover.
Had an uneventful journey of about 2 hrs. and on arrival sought out a canteen
wherein to consume Joyce's sandwiches supplemented by some tea. After a very
brief glance at the remains of the city we caught a connection to Goslar, which
fairly crawled along. As the names on the stations grew longer and more obtuse, so
the line got steeper and the townships smaller. We arrived at Goslar at 19.40 hrs
to find it a very wide, open air sort of little place on the edge of Harz, backed by
great slopes covered with pines.*

*A bus took us thence, via a road slightly reminiscent of some of my Rhône valley
peregrinations, to Hahnenklee. Hahnenklee lies in a slight dip high up in the
undulations of these pine forests that stretch as far as the eye can see … there is
none of the rather bleak bare rock I had expected. In the undulations also lie little
lakes, extending right up to the edge of the valley itself. The place is about the size
of Radlett, built virtually entirely in wood and mostly along chalet lines. It's very
clean and bright, of course, and the air is wonderfully soft and mild, but quite
breezy. The whole effect is a warm, pleasant one recalling doll's houses in picture
book scenes.*

*There is very little evidence of the military – 'Woodchopper' units are operating
locally, but the only establishments here are the O.R.s rest hotel and that at which
we are staying. This is an ex-hotel (as is one building in three hereabouts) with
about 20 guests – I am the only RAF bod. We have a nice double room and four
excellent meals a day served with a quartet for dinner – cost about 13/6d net per
diem.*

*Well – no more for now: the weather is terrifically hot immediately one moves
anywhere out of the breeze, and we are already quite tanned … I wish you were
here so that I might see that familiar lobster hue appear once more!*

Yours aye, Dick

Friday, 9 May

Rose at 09.00 hrs and had a good breakfast. This morning we strolled round the village, inspecting the shops with an eye to possible souvenirs. Then we wandered around one of the little lakes by the village – and found frogs literally by the hundred. It made me quite upset at seeing so much biological experimental material that I could not use ... and gave rise to much fruitless speculation as to their financial value at 6d net!

Joyce by 'Frog Lake' on the first morning

After lunch it was too hot to attempt anything rigorous – I did an hour's pathology, whilst Joyce slept. Had a piece – only one piece, alas of a lovely cream cake for tea, then a walk through the woods.

Saturday, 10 May

Weather today a little duller than yesterday, but still fine – we had another stroll through the village this morning and bought a couple of brooches etc. as souvenirs.

There was a dance at the Club this evening, but Joyce and I read in the lounge and

Joyce taking a stroll through the woods

took no more active part than going in to see the Cabaret before retiring to bed – a ventriloquist, dancer, singer and pair of jugglers whom we had already seen in action on the stage at Lüneburg.

Sunday, 11 May
After breakfast J and I set out with the binoculars and cameras to scale the biggest of the hills overlooking Hahnenklee. Once up there I scaled an observation tower and took a few shots of the view whilst a German on the ground hurled invective against me. Then, on descending I took further snaps of Hahnenklee, bright and diminutive in the sunlight below.

Rest of the day uneventful – I read, did some Path revision and wrote to Tim. This evening J and I got into conversation with one of the Army wives – there are several 'stranded here', awaiting the arrival of their husbands who are following from Italy.

Above: Goslar Town Hall   Below: Joyce in front of the observation tower at Harz

Monday, 12 May

Up early this morning (08.00 hrs) and went down on a TCV (troop carrying vehicle) to Goslar, to look round the town and buy some souvenirs. Though, however, it is an old and picturesque place, when I tried a few 'arty' angles in photography, its shops were devoid of anything worth buying. Joyce, too, feels the local natives are hostile and does not feel at ease hereabouts – I gather the area was one of the strongholds of Nazism.

Anzio Club
Hahnenklee

Dear Dad
Wedy. 13.5.47
18.00 hrs

Since writing last we have done little but ramble through the forests and lie in deck chairs sunbathing. On one occasion, the other morning, we took advantage of a truck going down to Goslar to run in and have a ramble round the old town – which has not been bombed at all. Despite this the people round here seem rather a surly lot, reluctant to give one any help in one's walks or shopping – the most definite anti-British feeling I have come across yet. I recall that it was at Brunswick, not far away, that the most serious of the recent rioting took place. Even amongst Germans, I have gathered from Joyce's Lüneburg friends, the people of the Ober-Harz have a reputation for surliness.

Over the weekend, and on some evenings, a lot of visitors flock into the Club – most of the time we have had the place to ourselves, sharing it only with some wives recently shipped out of Trieste [these are the wives of the officers on the staff of the British Brigadier de Winton who was assassinated in March] and awaiting their husbands who are en route to join them. So Joyce has not been hard up for someone to whom to gossip!

… So you can see we are leading the life of recluses … still, we are well away from all regulations and 'bull' and feel better for the change.

Yours aye, Dick

Tuesday, 13 May

We had planned a walk this morning, but some colicky abdominal pain of mine necessitated its postponement – I think I was unfortunate in my portion of fish cake yesterday at lunch, because since early today I have had a copious water diarrhoea. In an effort to relieve it I 'missed' dinner tonight and had only one motion in the evening – after a glass of lemonade. The ingestion of any food or fluid provokes an instant desire to go to stool – presumably a very sensitive gastro-colic reflex.

Wednesday, 14 May

Today chiefly noteworthy for my sufferings with the 'flux'. Was up twice in the wee sma' hours, and then took some opium and creta aromat. and slept well. But during the day – especially its latter part – had frequently to make abrupt dashes to the toilet – fortunately there is a wide choice here.

This morning though, felt fit enough to walk through the nearly village of Bockswiese and to inspect an abandoned tank beyond it. Took some photos of it – and of a local goat, whose owner cursed me heartily in German for standing on his grass. They are a surly lot hereabouts! Afternoon and evening spent reading, writing and doing my regular two hours' work.

Thursday, 15 May

Cloudy most of today – with occasional bursts of sunshine. Went down to the village to do some shopping but found today is observed as some sort of religious festival. Read, talked – alas – with Mrs M who is doing the loving wife act to the degree of inducing nauseation, whilst she waits for her blessed husband. The collection of married 'Army widows' here has occasioned J and I some amusement during our stay – they had been evacuated from Italy about 5 weeks ago, and are waiting for their husbands to follows.

Friday, 16 May

Again rather a dullish day – breakfast at 10.00 hrs and soon afterwards went down

Panther tank in the Harz Mountains
[Panther was the final production model, Ausf G, from 1944 onwards. Distinguishing features are delection of driver's vision port in glacis plate and provision instead of rotating periscope (evidently removed in the above picture).] It might have been from Panzer Regiment 16 that formed part of the 116 Panzer Division that retreated into the Harz Mountains towards the end of the war.

to Hahnenklee and bought some little wooden brooches for the Mill Hillians. Then back for lunch – I had a short stroll on my own thereafter, but spent most of the day consuming detective novels with occasional interludes from the Pathology book. My dysentery, if anything, rather improved today!

Hahnenklee

Dear Dad   *Saty. 17.5.47*

Pleased to hear that you have received some more instruments safely – I hope that ere long I will have a complete set for General Surgery. Already I have some that would have been invaluable at my last job, to say nothing of a complete outfit for Post Mortem work. Quite apart from the pleasure of owning one's own tools, there is obviously an all round benefit to be derived from the operator 'knowing the feel' of his instruments, particularly in the case of things like chisels etc. It is interesting to note how much better designed most of the German surgical gear is than our own – particularly anything involving optical problems, such as specula. This feature has impressed me repeatedly, even in the rather ersatz stuff one gets nowadays: on the other hand, materials, strength and finish, as you have commented, fall far short of English standards under prevailing conditions. Anything that is at all unique or heavy though, I haven't entrusted to the post, so you must wait to see my better class stuff. A lot of the items sent home – and postage is by far my heaviest outlay on them – must seem a bit repetitive, but none of them are bought simply through collecting zeal! A simple appendicectomy, as you probably know, can involve the use of a dozen Spencer Wells – and the number rises steeply as soon as you tackle anything complicated in a fat subject!

… I'm wearing a suit Joyce brought out with her at present – my best or 'second best' – it is in good shape. We pay 13/3d per diem per person (bed, breakfast, lunch, tea and dinner) … so much for your queries.

Saturday, 17 May

Had only a short stroll this morning, but this afternoon I went off on my own for about an hour and a half, having a long amble through the woods round here, and feeling very quiet and lonely most of the time.

This evening, being Saturday, was an excuse for a 'Dance Night', so dinner cost 4/6d cash instead of the usual 3/-. We didn't dance – preferring to sit and read in the lounge – but we went in to see a cabaret – mostly some indifferent chorus and dancing numbers, plus a soprano and a couple of jugglers. Probably the most interesting turn was a man simulating to a very fine degree, a robot.

'Joyce, hold the camera this way!'

Sunday, 18 May

Our last day at Hahnenklee – and, since it rained pretty heavily most of the time, we did very little. I sat about, rather bored, and feeling glad that it was time to go – I wanted to get back to my different hobbies and away from the place where the constant doling out of money for each meal seemed to make a really cheap holiday nevertheless seem expensive.

Went down to Goslar by jeep and there caught the leave train to Hannover. Transport (a TCV) awaited us at the station, and we had a comfortable, rapid trip to the Transit Camp – here we were quite efficiently installed in a double room at the Transit Camp, had a couple of cups of tea and retired to bed.

Monday, 19 May

Up at 08.00 hrs. I managed to get a truck to take us down to the station a little before the main party left, so we had a quarter of an hour to stroll round the shops – I visited the surgical shop I had found on the occasion of my first trip and bought a couple of instruments.

Then caught the Diesel to Lüneburg and so home, arriving in Reichenbachstraße about 13.00 hrs. I rang the 'drome and found that I had missed a couple of compound fractures last week: and that the PMO was paying a visit tomorrow. Went down this afternoon to collect my mail, cigarettes etc. and so back to develop a film.

Letters from Tim – he has used the morphia I gave him on a fatally wounded L/Cpl who was accidentally shot in his quarters. Must send him some more.

> *Dear Dad* *Monday 19.5.47*
>
> *… There are a few snaps enclosed herewith for Pam – I'm a bit disappointed in them because they were taken late on a dull day. And most of all, because I haven't got very convincing evidence that I really did go in the lions' cage. In my hurry I sadly under-exposed! Still, I'll send the rather poor print along later. You can at any rate see a lion!*

Tuesday, 20 May

Up at 08.30 hrs and up to SSQ at 10.30 hrs, to hang about until such time as the PMO, BAFO arrived – a heavily built chap with a broken nose, who rolled up in a very affable fashion, at about 11.30 hrs with Tonk in tow. He had a look round SSQ and then did a sort of minor sanitary round of the Airmen's mess and the Unit Form. He and Tonkinson had lunch with the Groupy. I fed in the Mess and wandered off home soon after.

Spent evening reading and developing a film. Then to bed, after packing up a few things for tomorrow.

Wednesday, 21 May

Ambulance picked us up about 09.20 hrs and deposited us at the Atlantic Hotel in Hamburg about 10.45 hrs. Booked a double room (11/6d per night) and then went out – to my usual instrument shops. Bought only a few indifferent tools and returned for lunch – out again thereafter and this time tracked down a good rangefinder by Leitz, at the exorbitant price of 400 RM – this necessitated a little transaction to raise the necessary funds. Tea at the Carlisle Club, and then walked slowly back beside the Alster to the Atlantic.

RH next to the Lombardsbrücke on the banks of the Binnen Alster

Had a quick Ginger Ale and returned to the Gansemarcktstr. to the Garrison Cinema there to queue up for David Niven's *Matter of Life and Death* – a film containing some good ideas in its amusing pictures of the life hereafter, but I felt they were inadequately dealt with. Back to our luxurious room, had some cold meats for supper and so to bed.

Warm pleasant day, which we much enjoyed.

Thursday, 22 May

Up at 08.30 hrs and had breakfast – quite a good one – at 09.30 hrs. Out immediately afterwards and round the shops. I bought some bacteriological slides (53 for 140 Mks) and went to collect my camera range finder. Also purchased a small transformer for 80 RM.

Back to the hotel for lunch, after which we dozed and read in our rooms. Then set out again, in search of a surgical instrument shop in Stein Str. Having made a few purchases, then we took some photographs and made our way back to the Carlisle Club for tea.

Playing in the ruins of Hamburg

Bridge and ruins in Hamburg

Friday, 23 May

Just up in time for breakfast this morning, then packed our luggage up and vacated our rooms. Before lunch we investigated the Hauptbahnhof sector of the city and, finding a YMCA there, had morning coffee.

After dinner we carried our (fairly light) luggage as far as the Carlisle Club in Ganse Markt and there awaited transport back to Lüneburg. Actually, since the ambulance was under repair, our vehicle took the form of a 3-tonner, but we had a fairly comfortable trip back.

Dear Dad   *Friday 23.5.47*

Just to let you know we are back in Lüneburg, at the end of our holiday, which concluded with three days in Hamburg. The weather was very pleasant and we enjoyed ourselves greatly wandering round the City. Contrary to what you may visualize, Hamburg is a very modern airy place, and three large lakes right in its centre give it an aspect which is a cross between Venice and a seaside town. Of course, it's pretty badly flattened out, and in parts you still come across crosses stuck in piles of rubble indicating that the casualties have never been dug out. I'm sending a few snaps I bought (tuck them away after looking at them, for I have no copies). Later I trust I will be able to forward some of my own inimitable representations of Hamburg scenes!

Saturday, 24 May

Went down to SSQ at about 09.15 hrs, but today being a general holiday, had little work to do. Went back to Lüneburg towards the end of the morning, paid the balance of my 100 cigarettes to the local animal fancier and brought back to the flat in triumph a lovely aquarium, immersion heater and nine tropical fish – Macropodus, Guppy, Siamese fighting fish, 2 clown fish and a Sword-tailed fish.

Some domestic excitement in Reichenbachstraße this morning, because F/O R apparently returned home drunk last night and 'beat up' his wife! F/L C wants me to take some action about it!

This evening J and I went to see a film about an Australian cattle drive – *The Overlanders* – simple, but rather too amateurish and naive in parts.

On my return home felt definitely 'queer' and retired early to bed – only to spend a miserable night vomiting and having diarrhoea. At last felt better and fell asleep.

The Chilehaus (Chile House) is a ten-storey office building in Hamburg. It is located in the Kontorhausviertel. It is an exceptional example of the 1920's Brick Expressionism style of architecture. This large, angular building is located on a site of approximately 6000m², spanning the Fischertwiete Street in Hamburg. It was designed by the German architect Fritz Höger and finished in 1924.

Sunday, 25 May
Stayed in bed till noon, in view of my disturbed night. Then up and did about 1 hr and a quarter's work this afternoon. About 19.00 hrs Trudie and her mother came to tea, to celebrate the former's 21st birthday last week. They stayed quite late – until about 23.00 hrs and then left. Very short day it has seemed!

Monday, 26 May

Weather look really promising this morning and lived up to expectations. So we had an early lunch (i.e. one at the time when other people have lunch) and went on a YMCA expedition to a sandy beach on the shores of the Elbe, about half an hour's run away. Here I had a rather sandy tea and relaxed in the sun in rather half hearted fashion. Many RAF families present … then back, arriving home about 18.30.

Lauenburg on the banks of the Elbe

Tuesday, 27 May

Back to work this morning – and the first thing I heard was that F/L W had died in the BMH at Brunswick, where he was taken yesterday. It seems that he developed infectious hepatitis last week and – from what I heard when I phoned Brunswick – I gather he developed acute yellow atrophy.

Life in 151 R.U.(A) however, seems to continue in a disconcerting way and one life seems to be a very trivial thing after all …

The remainder of the day was uneventful. Returned home, did a couple of hours' work – had a read, and so to bed.

Wednesday, 28 May

Uneventful morning. This afternoon had a note from Dad, saying Grace had been advised to go to Redhill for an operation so, at his suggestion, wrote letters of introduction for her to Donald Fraser – or, alternatively – Douglas Macleod – and sent them off.

Later this afternoon gave my usual hygiene lecture to the NCOs here, and then returned home. In the evening – Joyce was helping at a birthday party in the flat below until about 19.45 hrs – we went to the cinema to see *Cloak & Dagger*, a rather conventional secret service story.

Joyce helped out at a children's party in the flat below

Thursday, 29 May

Nothing much to do in SSQ, but had two 'pycho' cases to see. One, a sergeant going 'downhill' on alcohol, the other a sub-normal ?man repeatedly in trouble. The first seemed an intelligent type, worried about difficulties with his officers, and about the ? he recently caught, I think may improve on simple treatment.

Dear Dad   *Wednesday 28.5.47*

I've sent you the usual letter by ordinary mail this morning, so this one is concerned only with Grace's troubles as detailed in your note which I have just received.

It's a little ticklish to organize second opinions at this distance, on a case I know very little about, but this is what I suggest.

Frankly, I don't think Sophia's opinion is that much better than my own! So I've had a letter typed to Donald Fraser of Barts, who taught me, and who is a thoroughly capable chap. Very likeable fellow and quite young, and I guess he'll remember me and will help – Joyce had something to do with a broadcast of his. Unfortunately he may have left London before now, so – to save time if you get no answer from him (I don't think he's gone) – a second letter has been prepared to Douglas Macleod of the U.C.H. He's an older man, and one glance at the Directory will answer for him. Unfortunately the personal contact is much remoter, though I think he would co-operate.

I suggest you see Meek, tell him you have asked me about a second opinion. Then send off one of the letters – will you please address them? (There is a small initial in one corner of each envelope.) In the case of each specialist, you will receive a phone call one evening asking for Meek's address and fixing up the appointment etc.

… Trust Grace will survive all this negotiation unharmed, but you can assure her of the undoubted ability of whichever man she sees.

With best wishes to you & her,
In haste,
Dick

Friday, 30 May

A very hot sunny day: I took sick parade and gave my first-aid lecture to the Discip. Course. Then Tickner flew me off in an Auster to 123 Wing at Wundsdorf – had a nice trip down, about 40 minutes in the air. On arrival we had lunch and were then driven to the Military Cemetery at Limmen, just outside Hannover – the graves are on the side of a green sunny hill, surmounted by a flagstaff. A majority of them are RAF, many 'unknown', and it would seem that most of the bodies have been re-interred from other sites. Indeed, whilst we awaited the arrival of the body of F/L W, a truck drove up and unloaded some half-dozen tarpaulin wrapped 'packages' which were buried.

The cortège – six officers bearing the coffin, conveyed on a 15 cwt – arrived at about 15.30 hrs. An RAF chaplain read a not very lyrical service, the RAF Regt. fired three blank volleys and two Group trumpeters blew the Last Post, then Reveille. Tickner, myself and the pall bearers saluted the grave and 'Watty' had been committed to rest.

The funeral of F/L 'Watty'

Perhaps it was the effect of this ceremony, but I felt distinctly 'windy' during the flight back. Especially since Red Verey lights were fired as we took off and we had to land again – a forest fire at Lüneburg had caused them to decline our landing there. I could see Tickner was determined to put the kite down again at 151 and felt distinctly easier when we saw the field was, in point of fact, clear. Though there had, apparently been a local blaze, and we passed an even bigger one en route. Safe home for a quiet evening.

The flight in the Auster with Tickner at the controls

Saturday, 31 May

Weather still very warm – pretty busy morning on many odd jobs but arrived home fairly early for lunch. Went back soon after to 151, but the Gliding Club were only flying the heavier machines during the afternoon. So I went back to the flat and did an hour's Anatomy – more asleep than awake in the heat of the afternoon.

At about 19.00 hrs felt cool enough to make another trip to the airfield and stayed there about two hours. In this time I had two ground slides in the SG38 behind a jeep, and regained a little confidence. Came home feeling my 'A' licence was perhaps not so nebulous after all.

RH and Mosquito (FBV16)

think you will like

work and, with a warm

JUNE 1947

JUNE 1947

Sunday, 1 June
Probably the hottest day of the year so far – and, in consequence, I felt too hot to do anything useful most of the time. Managed to put in a couple of good hours on the books during the cool of the morning – after lunch sat about reading and later developed a film. At 17.45 hrs went up to the airfield again, intent on some more ground sliding; but the Primary trainer was u/s so I returned to the flat and 'wasted' the evening sitting about reading. Very warm indeed, even at the time (23.15) of writing this – J wandered round all evening in brassière and knickers!

Monday, 2 June
Quiet day, disturbed only by agitation about such things as an examination of the ambulance mileage etc. Worked before breakfast and – rather drowsily – this evening.

Tuesday, 3 June
Not much work to do today – got up at 07.10 hrs and studied until breakfast time. Then had a fairly quiet day in SSQ, during which I did a short sanitary round. I'm beginning to feel the need of a diversion of some sort, I would like to do some wireless construction. But the necessary scrounging round for every little component would be a hard job, and even after collecting them, such tools as a soldering iron would present virtually insuperable difficulties – still, I might have a try. Receivers have been built under conditions incomparably worse than those I enjoy!

Wednesday, 4 June
Another scorching day – had a very ordinary morning, but this afternoon took myself some time off and spent the best part of the rest of the day sitting out in the sun on the aerodrome with the gliders. Save for three quarters of an hour when I lectured the NCO's course – nominally on Hygiene, but actually on a couple of topics of my own choosing e.g. Benzedrine. Then back to the gliders: I had only one 'launch' all the time I was there – a ground slide where, once again, I was disconcerted to find myself suddenly airborne. This time, however, I acted more rapidly and got down again without a bump.

Grunau Training Glider

Home – after visiting two small patients of the 'chill-and-sore-throat' variety who seem so prevalent just now – and was looking forward to a quiet meal and a rest when Monica and Marga Heine arrived and, since a thunderstorm developed, stayed until after 23.00 hrs.

Thursday, 5 June

Wet, rainy and, thank goodness, cool, today. Fairly busy most of the time – couple of cases to visit, odd medicals to carry out etc. This evening Joyce and our neighbours went dancing and I put in a couple of hours on the textbooks; as usual, I tended to doze over the Anatomy notes, but had no difficulty over the Physiology, where I am beginning to feel that I now know at least 10 per cent of what I so effortlessly forgot three or four years ago. How I wish I had been able to persevere with Primary then – though, the incentive not being there, I doubt if my efforts would have met with much success.

Friday, 6 June

Pretty busy day, but nothing exciting. The morning I spent waiting to see if I would be called to give evidence at a District Court Martial, in a case of two sergeants charged with assaulting, whilst drunk, two airmen. Then had to scurry round this afternoon to make up for lost time: including a treatment of S/L P's ingrowing toenail – always a rather unsatisfactory sort of problem. I managed to pack the oedematous skin fold away from the nail edge under ethyl chloride. Wonder if Nupercaine on the wisps of cotton wool used for this job would make it a less painful one?

Dear Dad   *Friday 6.6.47*

... As in London, the weather here broke sharply on Wednesday evening: since when, we have had intermittent rain and low cloud. The hot weather has brought a burst of summer diarrhoea, mosquito bites and sore feet in its wake – I've now got a Group Captain and a couple of Squadron Leaders under my thumb, the Catering Officer in one of my beds and the O.C. Flying on my visiting list ... I begin to understand how the M.O. can become the virtual 2nd i/c of a unit – the actual Wing Commander is deaf and suffers with eye trouble, so I've controlled him months ago!

Tomorrow we are holding the rehearsal for the AOC's inspection in two weeks time – every manjack on the station lined up, 800 strong on parade ... I've been turning away malingerers for 24 hours now ... when I say every manjack, I except of course, one officer who, as befits his status, has permission to recline in the ambulance!

Thanks for news of Tim – when you drop him a line, tell him again that my letters will eventually follow him on from Jerusalem – I have written to him regularly, but some went by surface mail, and by a note from him received today I gather he had not heard from me for some time. Will be sending him an Air Mail this weekend. Where is Gaza, anyhow?

Well, no more for now – have been listening to 'D-Day' programme, after a day wasted hanging around a district court-martial in case I was wanted as a witness.

Pip-pip,
Yours aye,
Dick

Saturday, 7 June

This morning a Station Parade was held, as a rehearsal for the forthcoming AOC's inspection. Everyone was on parade at 8.45 hrs. I rose early and sat in my ambulance, just off the parade tarmac, watching for the first time the slightly 'off' drill of the RAF with their officers walking in threes up and down the edge – in a manner reminiscent of our school prefects walking round the The Large during morning assembly ... how long ago that seems!

Had a couple of cases to see later. A boy of ten I sent to Hamburg with a probable appendix – after watching him for 24 hours. Only today did he definitely show R.I.F. [Right Iliac Fossa] tenderness, though I felt that in hospital practice I would have seen him again late last night and opened him then. This business of weighing the pros and cons of a trip to Hamburg is often, I think, very dangerous.

This evening, a dance at the Officers' Mess – spoilt by an indifferent dinner, paucity of couples and too many rather sozzled officers.

Sunday, 8 June

As a consequence of last night's activities lay in bed until 11.40 hrs. Had to pay a visit to SSQ before lunch to dress S/L P's toe, but managed to get a couple of hours' work in later in the day.

Monday, 9 June

Started to rise early, but felt tired and cold on a grey morning and soon returned to bed. Usual daily routine at SSQ; gave a first aid lecture this afternoon, and then saw my usual bunch of expectant mothers.

This evening Jeanne and Bill 'the stage lovers' came to dinner and wearied us with their public courtship. We concluded that they suffer from a failure to mature emotional and sexual feelings to an adequate degree – for they have been married four years.

Tuesday, 10 June

To Monica Heine's with Joyce this evening. Home to listen to Mystery Playhouse and so to bed.

Wednesday, 11 June

Quiet morning – went down to Lüneburg to get some films printed and to negotiate the purchase of a 35mm enlarger.

This afternoon popped up to the airfield to get in a ground slide, and was pulled along with much trepidation on my part into a strong wind which threatened to precipitate me into the predicament in which I found myself when I started training. But towards the end of the tow found myself feeling more confident – and, when I saw another pupil going on one felt that my nervousness was, after all, ill-founded. I still have, however, an altogether baseless conviction that I'd feel far safer in a built-in machine instead of this SG38 affair.

This afternoon saw a girl aged ten with recurrent blepharitis – and noticed a small pigment spot in her other sclerotic which I take to be a melanoma. Present $1/12$ her mother says, but enlarging. Will await an ophthalmologist's report with great interest.

Thursday, 12 June

Quiet day –Joyce went out to initiate the local Guides for troop tonight, whilst I stayed behind and worked.

Friday, 13 June

The day at SSQ was so quiet that I was able to get out this morning and collect from Lüneburg some films and to buy some more fish – small Bridesveil – for our flourishing tank. Unfortunately immediately they had been added to our stock, one of the young fish was seized and killed by the big green and red Macropodius – which has always monopolised the food supply and has kept the Siamese fighting fish immobilised on the bottom behind a rock. So – rather reluctantly, because it was our prettiest specimen – I returned it to the shop and obtained a couple of tamer fish in exchange.

Did some work this evening – Group Anatomy reached me today from home – until the Heine sisters came round to coffee. Our tank seems to have a very considerable entertainment value!

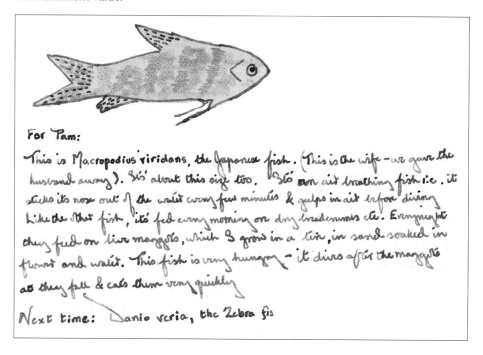

For Pam:

This is Macropodius viridans, the Japanese fish. (This is the wife – we gave the husband away). It's about this size too. It's an air breathing fish i.e. it sticks its nose out of the water every few minutes & gulps in air before diving like the other fish, it's fed every morning on dry breadcrumbs etc. Every night they feed on live maggots, which I grow in a tin, in sand soaked in flour and water. This fish is very hungry – it dives after the maggots as they fall & eats them very quickly

Next time: Danio veria, the Zebra fis

Saturday, 14 June

Overslept this morning – our alarm clock is temperamental – and did not take sick parade until 09.30 hrs. The rest of the morning spent organising next week's VD film.

Was going to try a 'low hop' at Gliding Club this afternoon, but the weather was showery, and instead went to the YMCA for tea.

This evening – after some Phys. & Path. – went to the cinema to see a film related – that is the best word, though the relationship was remote – to Dana's *Two Years Before the Mast* – much in the vein of a similar effort called – again quite erroneously – *Mutiny on the Bounty.*

Dear Dad   *Monday 16.6.47*

Had a very wet but pleasant weekend – went to the cinema here on Saturday to see 'Two Years Before the Mast' … any connection, unfortunately, with any book of that name being more imagined than real. Yesterday we went to see the SMO as arranged – found he had dug his toes into a really magnificent house on the Elbe banks. We went to the Opera as originally planned – four of us in the late Kaiser's box with its attached suite and lavatory (I'd always wondered how these things were arranged!) Very fine singing and orchestra of over sixty pieces but costumes and scenery, of course, along 'Austerity' lines. We spent the end of the evening in hospital reminiscences and returned by about 09.45 hrs this morning.

Nothing sensational today – I'm running a film cum lecture show, of a strictly pathological nature, for the whole unit this week and addressed the first section, 300 strong, this afternoon … pity my first public address should be on such an unsavoury topic!

Wednesday, 18 June

Quiet morning, spent the afternoon on the airfield and, under G/C Walker's guidance, accomplished two successful 'low hops' whilst being towed by the Jeep in our SG38. Returned home tonight feeling much more confident.

Thursday, 19 June

Up early this morning (07.45 hrs) to take sick parade before attending the CO's conference on Security Measures to be taken in the event of German strikes and demonstrations when the 'announcement of great importance affecting the level of German industry' is made. General note of reassurance and 'pooh-poohing' at the meeting, with mild alarms about the recent reappearance hereabouts of the old swastika symbol.

This afternoon fired my revolver course; the weapon is noisier and my aim less accurate than I had imagined. However, I scored a poor group, a passable target and boobed hopelessly on the Figure shooting.

Home and did some work – rather drowsily, for today was very hot – whilst J was at her Guide meeting. Then the end of the night was spoiled when the aquarium tank, heated by the sun, contracted as it cooled and sprang a leak.

Friday, 20 June

Had planned a trip to Hamburg today, but the threat of possible strikes and demonstrations deterred me – though actually the day passed off without any excitement.

Saturday, 21 June

This afternoon went up to the airfield and – after a long wait, because there were a lot of us and only a tractor available for recovering the cable – had a fairly lengthy and successful low hop. Home again immediately afterwards and did a little work and spent the evening reading – So to bed.

Sunday, 22 June

Our first anniversary – awoke at 10.00 hrs to hear man knocking on door with flowers for Joyce. Had breakfast together – had to go up to airfield for a short time this morning, but put in a couple of hours' work this afternoon.

'Birthday tea' early this evening with special cakes cooked by J. We went to the cinema afterwards and saw a Bob Hope style comedy – *The 5th Chair* – which suffered because

Bob Hope wasn't in it. So home, one short call-out, and so to bed. The events of a year ago are so fresh in my mind and my environment has changed so swiftly and often since, that only the indisputable evidence of the calendar convinces me that we really have been married one year!

RH and Joyce on the first wedding anniversary

Dear Dad   *1st Anniversary 1947*

We are having a quiet celebration today – Joyce has excelled herself in the culinary line and we're off to the flicks tonight. Had some cards from her relatives, a telegram from Ellis and another – rather vaguely – from 'the Milhillians': which? Our neighbours have a similar occasion (XIVth) tomorrow, so we are going to dinner with them.

Thanks for index cards and recent circulars … could you augment my library now with Samuel Wright's 'Physiology' which adorns one of your shelves.

Monday, 23 June

Rather a damp, dreary day – delivered myself of my usual lecture this afternoon to the Discip. course. This afternoon took the Married Families Clinic and then came home to do an hour's work before going with Joyce to the Colliers' downstairs – they are celebrating their 14th wedding anniversary today. Chicken and champagne supper – sat about talking till midnight, at which time I took a series of photographs of the Happy Couple and of ourselves (*see below*).

Tuesday, 24 June

Up rather earlier than usual for AOC's inspection – Air Commander Flynn came by air to tour the station, arriving at 10.00 hrs and starting with a detailed examination of the personnel on parade. I spent about an hour on the roof of flying control, taking photographs of the scene.

Rest of the day – save for a formal, unappetizing – luncheon spent hanging about SSQ awaiting the AOC's arrival. We had a fire practice during the afternoon – which, thanks to a faulty fire alarm system, was about five mins late. When the AOC finally showed up, about 17.20 hrs, he made a thorough but uninspired tour of SSQ and left without exhibiting any great interest in any of our activities, save possible the VD rate.

Home, and out to see Monica Heine – she and her sister were out, so we returned home and did some work.

Wednesday, 25 June

Rose early and did a rather 'rush' sick parade before leaving for Hamburg with J. There was an 'expectant mother' going up, so we were able to utilise a Volkswagen for the trip.

On arrival, having deposited the mother, I returned to the instrument shop in Colonnaden and made a few purchases – the instrument situation was rather poor – bought a few small items (e.g. 'aesthesiometer' needle and brush in a common holder) and a small transformer. Later in the day obtained a useful water bath, and a duplicate album for Tim. Had lunch at The Atlantic and bought J her 'anniversary present' – a scent spray and some lavender water. Then – after our usual cup of tea at the Carlisle

The home of the Heine sisters. Monica Heine was the SSQ Dispenser.

Club in Gansemarckt – returned to Lüneburg. In the evening I read, developed a film and felt too hot and tired to do any work – particularly since our water supply has been 'off' for over 24 hrs – due, I imagine, to the height of our flat and low pressure in the mains.

Thursday, 26 June
Another warm day – even more so than yesterday. Fortunately not much work – I spent some considerable time toddling round collecting odd wireless accessories, for I am now getting down to the idea of building myself a transmitter. Also gave M (Wing Commander) his medical – a real old regular, joined in 1914 or thereabouts, but now rather the worse for wear (due to nerve deafness and a possible specific iritis).

Friday, 27 June
First Aid lecture this morning – 'shock' for the umpteenth time – must try something fresh next week. Even my enthusiasm for lecturing begins to pall under this monotonous repetition. Spent part of the day scouting round collecting equipment for my new 'ham' station.

Knocked off early at 16.00 hrs after J had been up for tea and I had had one of my 'three cigarette' haircuts from the Station barber. Tried to do some work this evening and by taking a Benzedrine tablet managed to make a little headway against the drowsiness that steals over me on these warm evenings. Out to the Heine house for a short talk with Marga and back to bed.

Saturday, 28 June
A whole day's holiday on the unit today following the AOC's inspection. I had to go up to the unit once for a couple of Special Sick – RAF Regiment types trying to get off 'Jankers' for indubitably sore feet. Intended to go gliding, but when I had waited an hour on the baking hot airfield without even one launch taking place (cable trouble) gave it up as a waste of time and returned home to do some studying and put in a short spell on the wireless. Spent remainder of the day lying about the flat in very listless fashion – because of the terrific heat and the general symptoms associated with a mild URT infection.

A Neptune (Amphibian, Tracked, 4-ton General Service) entering the Hamburg Außenalster. The British officially named all the American built LVTs they used 'Buffalos' and the Neptune was a British vehicle designed for the same role. Few were built.

Had to go out at 00.45 hrs just as I was preparing to go to bed – a 'sprained ankle' which turned out to be a probable Potts#. Back half an hour later after splinting it up and so to bed.

Dear Dad   *28.6.1947*

Have had a note from Tim –nothing exciting, but he speculates on the possible chances of joining the battalion of the South Lancs which is in Austria. I sent his album off to you on Thursday, hope it arrives safely.

Yes, as you may expect, we are following closely the details of the Clements inquest – the case, of course, has a number of technical points which are of great interest to a doctor. But I agree with you that the whole affair is one scarcely calculated to raise the status of the medical profession in public opinion! (We get a free newspaper, 24 hours late, every day and spend Monday evening after dinner in an intensive study of News of the World, during which I enlarge Joyce's knowledge of forensic medicine. Incidentally, I see from the Lancet that Keith Simpson has recently published a textbook on the subject.)

RH's brother, Second Lieutenant A. S. 'Tim' Harrison, South Lancashire Regiment was serving in Egypt. Having failed to salute a very senior Staff Officer whilst meandering along holding a pile of towels, was immediately posted to Jerusalem. This was a hazardous posting in the aftermath of the bombing of the King David Hotel and the later abduction and murder of 'two sergeants'.

Sunday, 29 June

One of my most uncomfortable days yet – because it was so intensely hot and our rooms directly under the roof, soon become unbearable. Added to which I had an incipient cold. Joyce and I just lounged about half dressed, dozing or reading and feeling slightly irritable. Then to bed hoping that a faintly heard thunderstorm could move in our direction. Did, however, manage to complete my power pack – the first part of my projected wireless station.

Monday, 30 June

Fortunately much cooler today – busy day, including syringing the G/C ears and prescribing Scabies treatment for him and all his family. Bought an enlarger (35mm) today for which I have been hoarding the necessary for several weeks.

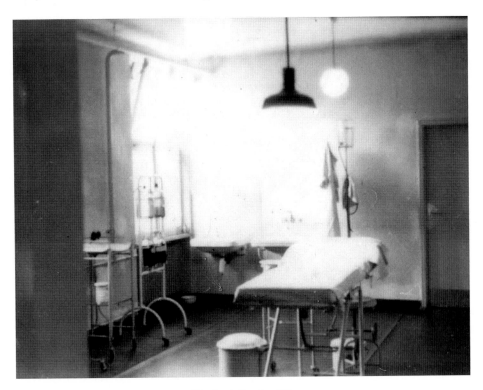

The Crash Theatre, SSQ

Meanwh[ile]
think you will lik[e]

work and, with a warm

R
Des[mond]

JULY 1947

JULY 1947

Dear Dad   1.7.47 Tuesy.

Pleased to receive your typed epistle of last weekend today, with all the current
intelligence … your previous remarks suggest that you have heard descriptions of some
pretty tense scenes in No. 33 – like yourself. I think it is unfortunate that Nan should
be exposed to such trouble. I note though, that you cannot refrain from adding that
the old lady *is* a bit tiring and still has a penchant for other people's concerns. I must
confess to sympathising slightly with Ronnie whilst regretting his behaviour!

Sorry to hear these vague rumours about Tim's 'rocket' – what were the details? Wish
he'd take his brother's example to heart – best of terms with everyone. Still, the most
fiery CO can't do much rocketing if he's dependent upon one for such homely tasks as
flushing wax out of his ears or treating his daughter for scabies!

Dear Dad   4.7.47 Friy.

Nothing to report – pleased to receive your note saying that Sammie Wright is en
route and that two of my parcels had arrived safely – hope that five more will follow
shortly, as follows:

> two boxes of instruments [cardboard]
> one box of instruments [wooden]
> one exposure meter
> Tim's album

Very quiet here – beginning to get hot again. Had a crash call today, but the machine
(certain mechanical failures) landed safely … which is more than can be said of
some other aircraft recently figuring in the Press, e.g. the York at Oakingdon, nr.
Cambridge.
Yours aye, Dick

Sunday, 6 July

Up at 10.00 hrs because J was going to Church. I did an hour's work this afternoon on Physiology, but devoted the bulk of the day to clearing up a series of outstanding jobs e.g. writing to Auntie Flo, putting a light behind the fish tank, etc. This afternoon had one short call to make and spent the remainder of the time trying to persuade my Xtal oscillator to oscillate – alas, unsuccessfully. This evening Trudie and her mother came round and ate the usual hearty meal. Had a bath and so to bed.

Weather very unsettled and alternating sunshine and heavy rain.

Monday, 7 July

Pretty hectic day with several odd jobs apart from routine ante-natal clinic and a VD lecture – my usual one the Discip. course given to an augmented audience. This afternoon, though, a second MO arrived … a quiet, very likeable sort of chap.

This evening bought and installed a small electric pump to aerate my fish tank; did two hours' work and at 21.00 hrs went out in the rain to phone Mill Hill. Had to wait an hour but eventually got through and had the scheduled three minutes (5/–) over the usually really good line – everyone (Dad and Grace) sound in good health and wishing me 'many happy returns'. Back to read *News of the World* over the Monday night coffee.

One's principal thought on attaining the age of 25 being one of regret of this period of 'idling' in the RAF when one should be pushing on to some useful training and towards a postgraduate qualification. Still, I suppose even BAFO life teaches a doctor some lessons.

Tuesday, 8 July

My birthday – and had one of the most enjoyable ones for years. Up at the usual time, to open parcels from Daventry (belt and ashtray) and from Joyce – a unique and very amusing book on the humours of early photography. Then the Collier children came up to sing 'Happy birthday dear Doctor' and to bring me tobacco etc.

Uneventful but fairly busy day in SSQ – gave a lecture on Hygiene at the end of the afternoon, then home – house cleared for a small party – Colliers, Rushworths and my new colleague (F/O Foulds) with Kirkland, the Dental Officer. Spent the evening talking, but took some photographs. Party finally broke up about 01.45 hrs. Joyce and I tidied up a bit and so to bed.

After so many birthdays 'on duty' in hospital, one spent in a house of my own, with a wife to cook me a cake and make an event of the day, is an innovation and a very enjoyable one at that.

Dear Dad, Grace, Pam & Alice   *My birthday 1947*

This is just a wee note to thank you for all the good wishes contained on the little card which I received – most appropriately – today.

I had a most enjoyable birthday – a book from Joyce, a belt and ashtray from Daventry, baccy from some neighbours and a lovely leather blotter from one of Joyce's fraulines. In the evening the Dental Officer, our neighbours and a new colleague came in – latter is a very decent chap, six weeks in the RAF (I think he's the first officer junior to myself I've yet encountered!) and fresh from Glasgow University. He's attached here 'indefinitely' with the proviso that he'll be shipped off if a job elsewhere falls vacant.

Joyce made a magnificent cake – beautifully iced with the RAF Medical Service badge. (There have been no ear syringings carried out here whilst this project was under way, the necessary squirter being non-available!); and piles of sandwiches, vol au vents, jellies etc. – altogether a most successful evening.

The happiest part of the day, of course, from many aspects, is its significance as regards my financial assets … an increment of 12/6d daily is not to be taken lightly. And, in six weeks time, I should get another increase of 6/– daily, to a F/L's rate of pay. (Actually, this promotion takes about 6–8 weeks to come through, but is, of course, back dated.)

The birthday cake which Joyce decorated using an SSQ ear syringe

Wednesday, 9 July

Felt very tired this morning after a late night last night, but fortunately had very little work to do – went round to see the G/C and had a conversation with him on VD which he will insist on trying to present as a purely statistical problem, to be evaluated as such.

This afternoon, Unit Sports, attended by Married Families and much rain. The most interesting item being a couple of good 'Tug O Wars'. I ran in the Officers' 100 yards on a crowded track – even, I fear, had I been in much better training, a start of up to 30 yards for the older competitors (three of whom were placed in the finish) was too great to be made up in the short total distance involved. Rushworth did well, winning two second prizes.

Thursday, 10 July

Had a day off today in view of the arrival of Foulds, and went with Rushworth across to Stade – he was trying to scrounge some equipment to make up some deficiencies in his stores on charge. I was on the lookout for some radio odds and ends – most of which I found. Returned, however, somewhat dejected by the sight of great piles of valuable receivers, transmitters, etc. which had been piled up there, obviously awaiting 'scrapping'.

Dear Dad   *11.7.47*

... I had a trip yesterday by car to a depot over the other side of Hamburg (Stade), which was something of a holiday from the normal routine – just a visit to another unit, and nothing worthy of note. I hope I'll have a few more excursions now that I have a colleague to stand by in my absence.
Yours aye,
Dick

Saturday, 12 July
Quiet morning – Rushworth gave me a very elegant Graflex flashbulb holder when I brought him home at lunch time.

This afternoon it was a bit gusty for gliding – I spent the afternoon with Rushworth wiring the small cubby-hole in our front room, for use as a darkroom. Then I made up some developer, showed him how to use my tank and came back upstairs to do some wireless.

Had to go to the 'drome to see a 'special sick' and again later on for a bod with a very doubtful pleurisy. In between, however, put in a good couple of hours in the darkroom and produced a couple of elegant prints of Sylvia Rushworth on the beach at Lauenberg. To bed after a short read – Joyce rather annoyed at my neglecting her all day for the aforementioned hobbies!

Sunday, 13 July
The afternoon was devoted to photography, with another session on the enlarger in my new 'darkroom'.

Monday, 14 July

Nothing very exciting today – gave my VD lecture this afternoon as usual – one man found the address apparently so stimulating that he fainted soon after I started!

Today got my wireless transmission licence application signed by a Signals Officer – the more readily because he wanted some professional advice, having just married a German girl and having developed gonorrhoea whilst on his honeymoon!

Tuesday, 15 July

Nothing much today either – usual two hours' work this evening after which I put the finishing touches on my crystal drive stage.

Wednesday, 16 July

S.M.O. (S/L Tonkinson) came down this morning, to give a lecture on VD in view of the raised incidence in recent months. A few rather embarrassed remarks by the G/C (who is overcome by modesty where VD is concerned) and then Tonk gave his lecture – a very much better one than I had expected, well delivered.

Went gliding this afternoon – after two hours wait did a low hop with rather less of my usual nervousness than last time. Then home early and did about 2½ hours' work rather drowsily.

Thursday, 17 July

This morning went to Lüneburg to collect some 35mm film – from which it may be gathered that the day was a fairly quiet one from a medical viewpoint. This afternoon collected my amplifier chassis from the machine shop, but did not put in much work on that – or on my FRCS studies – this evening, because F/L Venn was running a Gliding session. Only half a dozen pupils were there, so I got three trips in – all low hops. Probably made some progress, but had a bit of a psychological setback on the second 'flight' for, in an effort to land lightly, I almost stalled the glider and got an unexpected bump on landing. Passed on a third trip and came home.

Old Crane (Altes Kran), Lüneburg. In use since 1330, it is worked by a treadmill and was used in 1835 to unload the first engine brought from England to run a German railway (Nuremberg – Fürth). The vehicle to the left of the horse and cart is a British Bren gun carrier.

Friday, 18 July

Foulds went off to Hamburg today, to investigate the Black Market, so I was on my own – uneventful day. J came up for tea this afternoon. Evening on books, cleaning the fish tank and starting the construction of my amplifier. Saw a F/S with a loose nasal polyp hanging down his nostril and hadn't much idea what to do with it – am sending him to 94th on Monday.

Saturday, 19 July

Quiet morning – viewed a couple of VD films which are to be shown as part of our morality campaign. This afternoon stayed indoors doing wireless, save for one brief expedition to collect a sterilizer from the local instrument shop and to buy some photographic chemicals.

Sunday, 20 July

Up at 10.30 and put in a couple of hours' work this morning. This afternoon had a two-hour session constructing my modulation unit. By teatime, Joyce, as I'm afraid is sometimes the case over the weekend, was getting bored, and we had to go out for a short stroll. Upon my return I had a brief spell in the darkroom, but the results were not up to the standard of my first efforts and I soon got tired.

Monday, 21 July

Left SSQ at 09.15 hrs and went out with an RAF Regt. platoon to Lüneburg Heath, for an exercise shoot on trench mortars with live ammunition. Spent the morning before lunch watching the 3-inch mortars firing, being chiefly impressed by the noise of discharge and by the long time of flight (up to 25 seconds) of the projectiles.

In the lunch interval, went to the nearby Victory Hill to take some photos of the site of the surrender of the German Armies. Then back to eat a cold lunch – rather unappetising – out of mess tins and to watch the much less exciting 2-inch mortars in action.

RAF Regiment Mortar Shoot, Lüneburg

Dear Dad   *Wedy. 23.7.47*

Only to report I'm still alive and kicking – nothing to report. Had an uneventful weekend of quite warm weather. On Monday I went out for the day with the local RAF regiment who were conducting a 3-inch and 2-inch mortar shoot with live ammunition. This in itself was quite interesting, but the battle training area is within a few minutes walk of Victory Hill, on Lüneburg Heath, and during the lunch interval I was able to stroll over to have a look at the memorial there [see below].

Monday, 28 July
Up at 07.30 hrs and had a fair breakfast. Surprisingly enough, a TCV arrived on time and we proceeded to Hannover Station to board the Berlin train, which left at 09.21 hrs. From then on we had a comfortable compartment to ourselves, leaving it only for a good lunch in a clean and tidy dining car at 12.30, and for 'tea' (a cup of tea and a very small cake) about 16.00 hrs.

Soon after starting lunch we arrived in Magdeburg and saw some of our first Russians, in their peculiar flat caps, appallingly cut tunics and excessively baggy trousers. But at no point was the train boarded by Russians and we did not know at what point we crossed the frontier.

Berlin (Charlottenburg) at 17.05 hrs after running in through Potsdam (where we glimpsed the ruined palace) and Grunewald. Proceeded on a short run round the town, via Kaiser Damm Str, and eventually located the Married Families Transit and Leave Hostel near the Olympic Stadium – to our dismay old Graham and his miserable wife and daughter seem to have left Hahnenkleee and taken this place over.

Out for a stroll round the few surviving shops in Kaiser Damm this evening.

Tuesday, 29 July

Up at 07.40 hrs this morning, but had, after all, a long wait for the CCG bus. When it came, however, about 09.45 hrs, we had a very interesting trip round the principal sights of Berlin in it – to the Victory Column for the Franco-Prussian war, up which I climbed in rather dysphoric fashion, to take some pictures. To the very impressive Russian War Memorial – next to the old Reichstag. Then down Under den Linden, to the Emperor's palace and past the ruined Technical College and the University which is just re-opening. Then we saw Alexanderplatz, the former Piccadilly Circus of Berlin and its adjacent Gestapo HQ. The most interesting visit, in my opinion, was to the Reich Chancellery, scene of hard fighting in the Battle of Berlin and the site of Hitler's air-raid shelter, near which his reputed body was found. At this stage in the proceedings, unfortunately, my camera jammed and I was denied some of my anticipated pictures. On to the Allied Control Authority building and the unscathed Luftwaffe HQ.

After lunch Joyce and I went on a long, dusty and very hot shopping tour of Kaiser Damm Str and the Kaisershop. We didn't even do very much shopping! By the time we'd finished, had some tea in a Red Shield Canteen and dinner at our hostel, we felt unfit for anything except reading and writing a few postcards this evening.

BERLIN (RH original captions)

Russian Victory Memorial
Tank on the Russian war memorial. The ruined Reichstag in the background. (They say the instigator of
the burning, Goering, disclosed his identity by leaving his dog behind. Its body is said to hang from the
rafters still

Built in seven days with marble from Reichs Chancellery. The Russian soldier points at two black marble
slabs, under which lie the bodies of five officers and five ORs killed in the Battle of Berlin.
The guns are the first to fire on the city: the tanks (top photo) the first to enter it

Garden entrance to the bunker, Reichs Chancellery. The two towers – one unfinished – protected the entrances of the air filters. In this garden, Hitler took his only exercise during the last weeks of his life

Entrance to Hitler's bunker, at which his reputed body was found. Parts of the air conditioning system (Trevor Roper's book) seen in foreground

The Reichs Chancellery – main hall, with gold inlaid mosaic floor

Gestapo HQ, Alexanderplatz

Wednesday, 30 July

Left the house at 09.45 hrs today and went by CCG bus to Hohenzollerndamm where I visited an address given to me in a chemist's shop yesterday – the chap turned out to be a surgical instrument dealer with a really luxuriant stock. My day was spoilt by being unable to buy a beautiful cystoscope set, ridiculously cheap at 500 cigarettes. As it was, for 300 and a pound of coffee, I obtained a set of duplicates for much stuff I already possess.

This afternoon Joyce and I bought family souvenirs; we came back home for dinner then went to see a YMCA amateur company play *A Murder Has Been Arranged* by Emlyn Williams. Fair acting and an exciting plot but one expected more from Emlyn Williams than a falling back upon the supernatural as a climax.

Thursday, 31 July

Rose at 08.30 hrs and, one hour later, set out in the CCG bus for a repeat performance of the Berlin tour. This time I took more photographs. I got the ones I wanted of the Chancellery and scrounged a couple of pieces of mosaic from the floor of the main hall.

The pieces of mosaic taken from the Chancellery and a charred cartridge case

The entrance of the Reichs Chancellery. This building was not damaged by bombing but was the scene of hard fighting in the last phase of the Berlin battle. The small balcony was often used by Hitler for personal appearances

In addition I think J and I appreciated and enjoyed the tour even more at a second attendance.

Afternoon spent on odd shopping – paid a repeat visit to the instrument seller, but this proved abortive because he was out.

This evening visited a local cinema to see Humphrey Bogart in a not-extraordinary 'I've been framed' sort of murder mystery – *Dead Reckoning*. So back to bed feeling, as usual, pretty hungry.

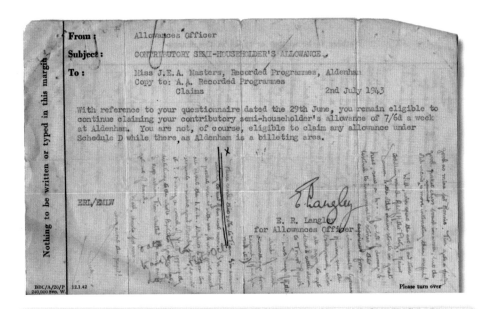

Dear Dad   *Thursy. 31.7.47*

Please excuse the old bit of paper [see above] J has just found for me – I'm writing in our bedroom and don't want to go across the road to the Mess for a more appropriate piece!

... Berlin, as you know, is divided into four sectors (British, USSR, USA, France) all standing in the Russian zone. We had a fine tour by motor coach the day after we arerived, round all four sectors, and a fine mess the whole show is. Literally not a single building of any size undamaged (except, strangely enough, the ex-Luftwaffe HQ). A few, however, have been patched up very well and hold, for example, a four-storey NAAFI club: Mil Gov. HQ and the Allied Control Authority.

I've pooped off a lot of film: unfortunately after an orgy at the Reichstag, Under den Linden etc., film gave out just after reaching the Chancellery, scene of Hitler's suicide and site of discovery of his reputed body. So Joyce and I went on the tour again this morning and this time snapped it all in extenso. Hope you'll see some good results soon.

Shops pretty empty – black market apparently flourishing. I've got a few poor souvenirs for you all – Pam's is perhaps the best; and an opthalmoscope almost as good as mine for Ronnie.

AUGUST 1947

Friday, 1 August

Spent this morning in desultory shopping in the Kaiserdamm – notably I purchased a masking frame and a couple of developing dishes. Back for an early lunch and then went down to Charlottenburg station for the 13.15 hrs train. This left punctually, after we had seen various OPs trying to persuade the RTO to allow them to board it.

Rather a weary journey, with frequent stops, in a full, but not overcrowded, carriage. Boredom relieved by two meals – tea and dinner – in the restaurant car.

Arrived in Hannover about 23.00 hrs and we were conveyed to the now familiar transit camp by a TCV and given a comparatively luxurious room with four beds! Tuned in my MRC, had some tea and cakes and so to bed.

Saturday, 2 August

Up at 08.30 hrs and had breakfast, after which I set out on my own to hitchhike to Hannover for an unproductive prowl round the instrument and photographic shops there.

Returned for an early lunch; then Joyce and I were taken down to the station where we caught the 13.15 hrs train home – arrived about 16.00 hrs and went up to SSQ to find out what had happened in my absence. Actually a few more cases of poliomyelitis had occurred – still amongst the German population – and a Polish watchman had shot himself.

Spent the evening developing the first reel of my Berlin films. Very pleased to receive

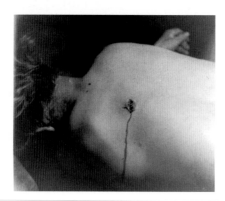

Polish watchman.
Luneberg. Germany. July. '47.
Suicide — ·303 Service rifle,
fired whilst sitting on edge of
bed, with big toe on trigger.
Instantaneous death.
[Exit wound shown].

by transmitting licence – my call sign to be D2 HC. Did a little work accordingly on my 'rig' and so to bed, after giving F/O Foulds (en route for a weekend in Berlin) a cup of coffee.

Sunday, 3 August
Did not get up till 10.30 hrs – by the time I had been to SSQ to look at a couple of cases then the morning had gone. Spent the rest of the day in an hour's work, writing letters and, after doing a little photography, I am rebuilding part of my Xtal Oscillator. Warm day, nothing very exciting.

Dear Dad   *Suny. 3.8.47*

Returned home quite safely yesterday afternoon, having had a pretty comfortable trip from Berlin to Hannover on Friday, and having spent that night in the transit camp at the latter place.

All seems quiet on my return – there have been half a dozen more polio cases in the last week, but the British personnel are still unscathed. As usual I missed the one exciting interlude of the last three months – Polish watchman on the aerodrome committed suicide by shooting himself through the chest with a rifle!

Pleased to find a big pile of mail awaiting us – from Ronnie reporting heavy responsibilities and a gratifying influx of most unpleasant cases from the Westmoreland County Hospital, Kendal, where he is doing a vacation job as H.S. (unqualified). One from Tim, writing from Suez but without any more details of his job with the K.A. Rifles than you've already supplied. Like you, I'm relieved that he's away from Jerusalem, and I trust he'll keep himself out of mischief in E.A. I gather he's now a first class shot (rifle) and marksman (Bren).

Pam will be interested to know that Joyce has just been given a dog – a puppy aged about six weeks, a bitch of the species usually termed 'dachshund' in England. (Actually a dakel, a dachshund being, properly, a hunting dog.) Will send a picture soon – it's a pleasant little thing.

RH with Denys the Dachshund puppy

Tuesday, 5 August

Back to work today – fairly quiet time; did a couple of hours' work this evening, then started on the construction of the final (PA) stage of the transmitter.

Wednesday, 6 August

Left airfield early this afternoon and, after a little shopping in Lüneburg with Foulds, came home to work, whilst Trudie, who arrived shortly after I did, talked with Joyce.

Then set about printing my final Berlin photos – much better than my first efforts, though I'm still having some trouble with accurate focusing of the camera and/or enlarger.

Trudie's mother came to dinner, after which I wrote to Dad, put in a little more work on the transmitter and retired late to bed. Note from Tim – still at Suez and awaiting a steamer to East Africa, where he is to be attached to the King's African Rifles. Poor chap – moving about on his own. Now, settled in a flat of my own and surrounded by my hobbies I am no longer conscious of being 'On Active Service' at all.

Tim awaiting transit to East Africa

Tim writing a letter on board His Majesty's Troopship 'Ascanius'.

Dear Dad   *Wedy. 6.8.47*

Pleased to have your weekend epistle today, accompanied by one from Tim – who is, by all accounts, thoroughly 'browned off'. I hope you will keep odd letters and forward them again as soon as Tim can give you a reliable address.

A few Berlin snaps are enclosed herewith – not by any means the best I took, but the only ones I've had a chance to develop and print. Some rather more interesting ones are drying out at the moment, and you'll get those at the weekend.

The palace 'Sans Souci' of Frederic the Great at Potsdam

Friday, 8 August

This evening – after a peaceful day – went with J and F/O Foulds to the local cinema to see Ralph Richardson in *School for Secrets* – the tale of the development of Radar. Very interesting but – to my admittedly biased way of thinking – not technical enough and a bit too full of the 'human interest' side of the picture – a bit more authentic detail and background would have been appreciated.

Saturday, 9 August

Very quiet morning – home rather late, having been to collect from stores an AR88 to serve as an RX for my station.

Did an hour's work this afternoon, and from then on the day was devoted to finishing my PR stage and testing my transmitter – gratified to find that it worked to the extent of transmitting speech across the flat, but rather disappointed by the feeble quality of its output. To bed in a tolerant and satisfied mood.

Sunday, 10 August

Rose at 10.30 hrs and spent the interval before lunch doing some Physiology revision and writing some letters.

From then on the rest of the day was devoted to servicing the transmitter – now that its construction proper is completed I am possessed, after building it fairly leisurely, by something of a fever to get 'on the air'. Unfortunately, though we (Foulds and Rushworth came up to collaborate this evening) succeeded without much difficulty in putting out a well modulated and definite signal, it was so weak that only with difficulty could it be heard on the ground floor! To bed, still quite optimistic but rather more subdued than last night.

Wednesday, 13 August

Got my revision done by 16.30 hrs and then took J to the YMCA for tea. Home and after dinner – to my wife's disgust – set about trying to bolster up my signal output on the new TX, still further. To bed about 00.30 hrs in a distinctly chilly atmosphere.

Dear Dad   *Tuesy. 12.8.47*

I'm sending you a note for onward transmission to Tim, and trust that you'll be able to make up a pile of any of my returned letters and send those off in addition at some later date. I had a letter from him yesterday (the very frequency of these missives indicates his idle state!) and as usual he was 'binding' about poor mail and nothing to do. Hope he'll find himself on a good posting in Africa – I always imagined the KAR was something of an élite corps. Certainly he doesn't seem to have been as happy with his own regiment as with his native levées – the change, I expect, was similar to that experienced by me when I left the free and easy life of the Rhône chain for the 'bull' laden atmosphere of BAFO.

Hope Alice had a comfortable trip to Yorkshire (who is this Miss Hawley anyway?) I'm very glad I didn't listen to the news bulletin on Saturday night, because I was under the impression that she was travelling that day. I might have felt a bit worried about the time of the train concerned had it been announced.

As for your query re our dog – well, a bitch was the only one available from the particular litter at our disposal. Still, I think the environment in our flat is a suitably cloistered one. (I doubt if you'll ever see this remarkable hound – quarantine expenses, I gather, are absolutely prohibitive.)

No signals from Radio Harrison yet – I've transmitted quite effectively from top to bottom of our house, but I'm still engaged in matching the set to a suitable external aerial.

Well, pip-pip for now,
Yours aye,
Dick

Denys the Dachshund

Thursday, 14 August

Foulds went off to Hamburg for the day so I had SSQ to myself – nothing very interesting turned up, save possibly some anal condylomata. Home and did two hours' work – then, after dinner, since J went out with Mrs Collier, I had a short period with the TX and, by modifying the modulator unit, got a rather better speech output. Felt even optimistic enough about things to consider going on the air this weekend, though the output is definitely 'low power' and the 7Mcs band very crowded.

Friday, 15 August

Foulds in bed all day with dysentery, albeit appearing very cheerful and not apparently gravely incapacitated.

I had a fairly fully occupied time in consequence, and – since J came up for tea – did not get back home until just before 18.00 hrs. Then, for the umpteenth time, tried a transmission test – this time with 0200 (Mike Noble). I received him well, but he failed to get any of my signals.

Somewhat disheartened I settled down and did about ¾ hr Physiology before – aided and abetted by brother Rushworth as usual – playing about with the TX. By reversing the modulator transformer I stepped up the speech output a bit and felt confident enough to send a CQ call … to no avail.

Saturday, 16 August

Unexciting morning – I went in unavailing search of a carbon microphone transformer. This evening and this afternoon was spent 'on the land' in unavailing search for a first QSL. At one stage in the proceedings I went out in the dark with the MRC receiver – pre-eminently suitable for this sort of job – to monitor the transmission. The set seems to put out a good quality signal, which admittedly tends to fall off a bit in a short distance. No joy on the band, anyhow – to bed rather frustrated.

These experiences were shared by F/O Foulds who came to supper and slept in the flat overnight.

Sunday, 17 August

Worked this morning – printed some films this afternoon and this evening again pressed on with the TX microphone. Had a call from TQ.O.AX and believe he heard me, but so poorly that he could not repeat my call sign. Cannot possibly call my first QSL. Rather dejected by this repeated failure.

Altes Kaufhaus, Lüneburg

Monday, 18 August

Dull day – tonight climbed onto the roof with Rushworth and, at this dizzy height, set about rigging an aerial on the roof, for it seems that my original quarter wave doublet is being very effectively screened by its proximity to the house.

Tuesday, 19 August

Went up to Hamburg today in a Volkswagen taking Mrs Sloane up for admittance for gynaecological investigation. Arrived in the city about 11.30 hrs. I went to Schrattscheider and bought a couple of instruments – later, after visiting R – to buy some foreign stamps for Tim. Not a very profitable morning, but collected some new instruments and some useful photographic accessories this afternoon, returning to Lüneburg about 17.30 hrs.

Foulds went with us to the cinema to see Alastair Sim in a 'juvenile comedy' *Hue & Cry* – a story about children solving a crime racket rather along the lines of *Emil et les Détectives*. After this most enjoyable film – embodying some most unusual and amusing characters – we stayed up talking so late that Foulds eventually spent the night here.

RH's own personal Volkswagen Beetle

Thursday, 21 August
Typical sort of day with no professional commitments. Diagnosed a case of herpes and photographed it – hope I thereby redeemed myself a little in Fould's eyes for a recent really florid case of rickets with bronchitis and gastro-enteritis which I blithely sent to 94th 'for diagnosis'.

St Nicolai, Lüneburg

Sunday, 24 August

Spent the morning working, writing letters and playing about (still to no advantage) with the transmitter. This afternoon we went for a walk (or rather, a 'dawdle' because we took Denys the Dawg along as well) to SSQ. Back about 19.00 hrs and I spent the evening reading and experimenting in colour-toning some prints – a chrome containing bath gives a very attractive stereoscopic effect and I envisage using it in future fairly extensively.

Monday, 25 August

Today, for the first time in my service career, I preferred a charge against a man – a member of the RAF Regiment who twice returned a thermometer placed in his mouth with a temperature of 110°F … and a cracked bulb. He complained of earache and had no physical signs.

Having one of my periods of 'Teaching Hospital nostalgia'.

Joyce at the market place with Denys

Joyce with Denys outside the Army Kinema Corporation theatre

Tuesday, 26 August

Uneventful day – collected suitable parts for a Power pack to form part of the revised TX. Tonight did two hours' work and then after dinner commenced the assembly of the 500V unit, my highest voltage outfit to date.

Dear Dad   *Thury. 26.8.47*

Still warm here, but no more scorching days at present. Poliomyelitis cases continue to occur but, as in the UK, there has been a sharp decline in the rate of incidence.

One point has recently occurred to me in connection with the host of robberies and burglaries which go on hereabouts – could you enquire from your pals about a suitable insurance. At present I am quite uncovered … I imagine our property is worth about £150–200, and the chief risks to consider would be theft and loss in transit – a very common occurrence here. I would be grateful if you could give me advice about a good policy.

Wednesday, 27 August
Off early this afternoon – two hours' work, tea at the YMCA and then spent part of the evening developing a film – with, alas, little success because air bubbles spoilt some of the best shots. To bed profoundly disappointed.

Thursday, 28 August
Most exciting event of the day was tending a woman having a miscarriage at 4–5 months. Foulds and I went down to see her and gave her some ergometrine whilst I expressed the placenta. We subsequently spent a long time photographing the foetus, and I arrived home too late to do much work.

Spent the evening printing last night's film – pleased to notice a marked improvement in focusing of detail, but this time had trouble with a very contrasty developer!

Lüneburg SSQ

Friday, 29 August

Fairly busy day – nothing outstanding. J left about about 14.30 hrs to take the Guides to a camp at Schleswig-Holstein and from now until next weekend I am on my own. It seems strange being a 'bachelor' once more, and, though I miss her and the evenings will seem long, it's pleasant to be able to arrange one's own meal and bed times! Spent the night putting in a good two hours' work and developing another film – this time with some of the most gratifying results to date.

Joyce's Girl Guides

Dear Dad   *Friy. 29.8.47*

I'm just commencing a bachelor's walk – Joyce left today, in her official capacity as a Lieutenant of The Guides to take her patrol to a camp in Schleswig-Holstein, about 80 miles from Hamburg on the shores of the Baltic. I'll continue to live in the flat but will probably take most of my meals in the Mess.

ABOVE: Lüneburg Old Harbour

BELOW: Children opposite Altes Kaufhaus, Lüneburg   OPPOSITE: Officers' Mess, Lüneburg

Saturday, 30 August

Had lunch in the Mess, but had to make a hurried departure thereafter to see if Mrs G really *was* in labour – she wasn't but slight indications justified her despatch today to Hamburg.

Then back to the flat and out to take some pictures of Lüneburg, for the Retina is at last beginning to give good results as regards focusing – perhaps a consequence of the use of a new (Glycin) developer. Intended spending the evening doing some prints, but Foulds asked me to go to the cinema – Somerset Maugham's rather vague *Razor Edge* – long rambling and rather pointless film. Home and 'tired the stars with talking' going to bed at 03.00 hrs – and even then pausing to take some time exposures of the moonlight!

Sunday, 31 August

Foulds and I rose just before 10.00 hrs and cooked our own breakfast of fried tomatoes. Then he returned to SSQ, whilst I wrote letters, did some work and had a short session on the new TX construction. Just before lunch had a visit from one of the German mess servants asking for my advice in the treatment of his father who has been three years in the hands of the Russians and is in a correspondingly poor state. Lunch with the Colliers.

Evening spent in a heavy aroma of gin from Rushworth whilst I printed some of my best negatives to date – pictures of Lüneburg. So at about midnight, to bed.

Meanwh[ile]...

...think you will like...

...work and, with a warm...

R Dev[...]

SEPTEMBER 1947

SEPTEMBER 1947

Monday, 1 August
Pretty busy day – but, as usual, nothing exciting. How differently the diary read eighteen months ago, when every day was marked by some new case or some new attempt at operative surgery!

Home at 19.00 hrs and did two hours' work before cooking myself a meal of fried tomatoes – which seem to be my principal item of diet nowadays – and opening a tin of ration cake – which is very rich and very good.

Poliomyelitis still causing 2–3 cases a week here in Lüneburg. Last Wednesday first British case occurred – wife of an Army officer. We now have 54 German cases in Lüneburg, 35 more in the surrounding Kreis [district].

Dear Dad   *Tuesy, 2.ix.47*

Had another note from you on Sunday, enclosing Alice's negatives, which will duly receive my attention. I'm returning your others herewith plus some of my variations on them … I took the liberty of cutting one to try it on my enlarger, and trust no one desired any further contact prints from it. Father doesn't appear in the enlargements because the bigger he got, the worse he looked!

Am fending quite well on my own and to date have suffered neither starvation nor dyspepsia. Joyce will be back on Saturday. Incidentally, her mother's birthday is on the 8th. Could you send a line (or wire)?

Thanks for some recent advertising matter and the latest 'Turtox' … which latter contained yet another contribution (on the Roof of the Frog's Mouth) from the pen of that distinguished savant, R.H.

No more news for now – must write Judda a pre-nuptial note.

St Michaelis, Lüneburg

Wednesday, 3 September

Stroll in town this afternoon – then some work. Dinner of a curry Mrs Collier sent up and spent remainder of evening finishing PA stage of Tx, before Rushworth came up and, waiting for his wife to return from Scharbeutz, kept me talking till about 01.00 hrs.

Thursday, 4 September

Busy day – Mrs B had intermittent abdominal pains and I had to visit her three times to try to exclude threatened abortion – finally gave her ¼ morphine and hoped she'd sleep it off. An accident case – laceration of ankle which I diagnosed as a dislocation – probably, in retrospect, erroneously. Visit to Julia Rowlinson who had diarrhoea after her camping trip.

Two hours' work this evening, then fried myself a 'mixed grill' and opened a tinned treacle pudding. Wireless work curtailed by the visit to Mrs B, but connected up the new PA stage and found that it more or less functions. So to bed at midnight.

Friday, 5 September

Another day during which I was pretty fully occupied – Mrs B fortunately less 'threatening' with less pain. Gave a first aid lecture to RAF Regiment this afternoon – tonight did two hours' work and then, with Rushworth as background, had a thoroughly successful evening experimenting with the transmitter.

Dear Dad   *Fridy, 5.ix.47*

Still leading my bachelor life or, as they say in German 'strohwitwer' (straw widower – peculiar, isn't it?) Joyce is due back on Sunday and is, by all accounts, working very hard with her tribe of girls. Anyhow, the weather is still very good for her and I gather the camp is proving a success.

No further word from Tim … I suppose the next note will be from Nairobi. I've had quite an energetic week, my opposite number being absent on leave in Berlin.

Fridy, 5.ix.47 continued …

Added to which a detention barracks has been established here, with all the prisoners to inspect, and the usual bunch of malingerers to sift through. This detention barracks too, is quite a place – barking of orders, everything scrubbed with sand until it's white. Had a nice compound fracture brought to us yesterday, too.

Yours aye, Dick

Saturday, 6 September

J rang up from Hamburg – sounding 'all-in' after a camping holiday that has been, I imagine, anything but a holiday for her – she's had to run, I gather, almost the entire outfit, and has probably had to 'rough it' for a week in a manner which usually sated *my* appetite for open-air life in about two days!

The Girl Guide camping holiday

The Girl Guide camping holiday

Sunday, 7 September

Rose at 10.45 hrs. Did an hour's work this morning – lunched at Rushworth's and then had to go out, just as Joyce returned, to stitch an airman's scalp wound after a car crash.

Home – toned a few prints, but had to go out with J to collect Denys from the Colliers, so rest of evening spent to very little avail.

Monday, 8 September

Only interesting event of the day was a very displaced # (fracture) radius and ulna in a young girl, which I reduced under $CHCl_3$ 'analgesia'.

Dear Dad   *Suny, 7.ix.47*

Joyce is due back this afternoon, and rang me last night from Hamburg, when the patrol stayed overnight – she sounded pretty tired and as far as I can gather, most of the other women nominally running the camp went off on various social occasions throughout the week, so that the greater part of the labour involved in looking after the fifty-odd Guides has been thrust onto poor Joyce!

I've done a couple of prints for Alice and forward them herewith, with a specimen or so of my own efforts. There are a couple more stamps here for Tim. And a copy of the first 'fizzer' I have instituted … the gentleman concerned being so foolish as to return a thermometer, previously inserted in his mouth, reading 110°, with its bulb cracked. When I took his temperature under observation it was 97° … but on the first occasion he'd been left by himself and was sitting next to the sterilizer! Keep it for my archives!

Tuesday, 9 September

Quieter day today because Foulds was back to share the labour. Nothing very exciting … worked this evening on the transmitter, still on the same problem – why the PA will not draw current when coupled to the aerial … a problem which the RR&I Squadron this afternoon were able to throw singularly little light on. Results still unsatisfactory – to bed disgusted.

Wednesday, 10 September

Off early – rainy day. Did an hour's work and then had a stroll round Lüneburg. Home, wrote up some journal abstracts and took J out to tea at the YMCA. Then rebuilt the last stage of the Tx – still to no avail!

Thursday, 11 September

This evening was settling down for another – presumably useless – evening on the radio, when Foulds visited us – and, since he was still here long after midnight, stayed the night.

Friday, 12 September
Joyce came up to SSQ for tea. Developed a film tonight.

Saturday, 13 September
Very warm, spent the afternoon wandering round Lüneburg with Skirly taking pictures, and the night developing films and reading and listening to the radio programme 'Battle for Britain'.

Clouds over Lüneburg , photographed from flat, September, 1947

Sunday, 14 September
Rose at 10.30 hrs and breakfast as usual. Had an emergency call at 11.15 hrs saying that the liberty run to Hamburg had overturned at Winsen. Foulds picked me up in one of the ambulances – we did 55 mph most of the way, and arrived at the scene at about 11.50 hrs. Found the 3-ton Thornycroft lying on its side – it had originally turned upside down after a skid – and one badly shocked man with a back injury still

at the roadside. Sent him to the 94th BMH and then proceeded to the nearby German hospital. Here – in a very shabby, dirty little establishment in a side street – we found the body of a Corporal – dead with a compound shattered # of the mandible and probably a fractured base: a case of fractured ribs, a laceration of the thigh, broken arm and a fourth man – K, one of our old thorns in the side on sick parade – with a # upper one third of femur. Our ministrations mostly devolved into injections of morphine and a rapid despatch to Hamburg. Then we moved the body to the mortuary and I returned to Lüneburg, passing two more cases en route for the 94th as I did so.

Rest of the day quiet – I developed some films I'd taken during the morning and tonight Foulds came down and stayed overnight – our usual chat went on until the wee sma' hours.

The fatal RTA at Winsen

Dear Dad   *16.40 hrs Suny 14.ix.47*

*Have had a very busy morning – emergency call just as I was finishing breakfast. The
3-ton Liberty Truck bound for Hamburg overturned 13 miles from here, finishing up
on its back with 21 men of 151 RV trapped beneath it – we sent all the five Lüneburg
ambulances, and the Army MOs followed Foulds and I out. One dead, and seven
seriously injured in Hamburg military hospital, five minor cases in Sick Quarters here
… I've just finished lunch. Bearing in mind <u>my</u> previous experience with a 3-tonner
and some tales heard since,* **I'm wondering if there's something radically wrong
with the vehicle.**

RH had survived an earlier
Thornycroft crash and had takien
this souvenir from
the wreckage

THORNYCROFT

TO MY DRIVER

Look after me, please, and treat me well.

Hundreds of men laboured hundreds of hours
to build me and I cost a lot of money. You
and your fellow citizens and comrades in arms
contributed towards my cost and if I am
neglected or damaged all this great effort and
expense may have been to no purpose.

Treat me well and together we shall serve our
country well.

Monday, 15 September

Busy day – heavy sick parade (due to the combined efforts of yesterday's crash and a
Battle of Britain parade scheduled for this morning). Had one good case – probable TB
(Haemoptysis and clubbing?) in an SP Sgt. Home early and spent the evening doing
prints. Letter today from Tim, who has arrived in Nairobi and seems to like the spot.

Tuesday, 16 September

Nothing remarkable today – spent over an hour with the CO – nominally discussing
the drafting of a VD report to the C-in-C but actually listening to his usual vague
theoretical projects in Public Health – a subject upon which he imagines, quite
erroneously, a sound practical outlook but in which he quite overlooks the importance
of a little technical acumen as well.

Wednesday, 17 September

This afternoon Mrs A came to see me in a great state – she had found a compromising note in her husband's clothes, foolishly written to his tall attractive typist. Mrs A on the verge of collapse. Promised to get the girl fired.

Thursday, 18 September

A fairly peaceful day – gave a lecture to the fire section, towards the end of it, however, I began to feel a bit squeamish and came home to experience a bout of diarrhoea. Felt so ill that I retired to bed and took a capsule of Nembutal. Quickly fell into a deep sleep.

Set about firing C – but A, who had unfortunately got wind of the whole business, interceded on her behalf and persuaded me to leave the job of getting rid of her to him.

Friday, 19 September

Awoke feeling very sleepy and distinctly 'woozy' from the effects of even 1½ grams of Nembutal. Stayed in bed until 10.00 hrs and then got up. Took some Amphetamine and went up to the camp to deliver a VD lecture.

Saturday, 20 September

This afternoon went down to the Married Families shop to buy Joyce some scent as a present for the 23rd and to interview the manager on the Rationing of Sanitary Towels! Very hot today – probably our last 'heatwave' day of this year.

Sunday, 21 September

Rose about 11.00 hrs. Did some work and took a few 'cloud' pictures this morning. Then – after the usual difficulty in finding the Volkswagen – went up to the camp to inspect the prisoners.

Home for lunch and then went for a long walk with Joyce to take pictures of Kloster Lüne, the Benedictine convent outside Lüneburg. Rather overcast weather, however, interfered somewhat with this project.

Kloster Lüne Convent

Kloster Lüne Convent

Monday, 22 September

This morning took advantage of some fine weather to have a short flight over Lüneburg and took some photos – also had a circuit over Lüneburg Heath and got worried when Muller flew very low on the return leg of the flight.

Got involved in a discussion on VD with the CO and had lunch rather late in consequence. Developed my (under-exposed) film this evening.

This morning wind and rain announced, in what looked a very definite manner, the advent of Autumn.

'Very low flight' over Lüneburg (arrow indicates No. 1 Reichenbachstraße – their flat)

Dear Dad   *Mony. 22.ix.47*

Thanks for your note of last week, describing Pam's first experiences of Education (? Where ?) and receipt of one of my heavier parcels of tools … we are now up to date, save for a bloodcounting set sent off last Saturday. This consists of a glass slide in a fragile Bakelite case, so I await a report of its condition on arrival with some trepidation!

Had another note from Tim yesterday, which I'm enclosing herewith – he seems to be fairly comfortable in his new job … has he any serious ideas as to his eventual niche in Civvy Street? He'll have to be careful, with all these prospects of direction of labour hanging over our heads.

We've had a quiet weekend – it started off with a heatwave, which, in the short space of last night suddenly waned. Today there's a fair wind and some rain, so that the scene has become intensely autumnal – a bright spell this morning enabled me to have a brief cruise over the town in search of photographs … a note of caution being introduced into the flight by my noticing a report of the inquest last week on a Mosquito pilot 'and his passenger, the Station Medical Officer!'

Tuesday, 23 September

The fourth anniversary of my meeting J. She gave me some hankies and braces – I gave her some scent and brought a few flowers home with me tonight. Spent a quiet evening – I printed some indifferent negatives, then took J on my knee as of yore. But she's a bit heavier now!

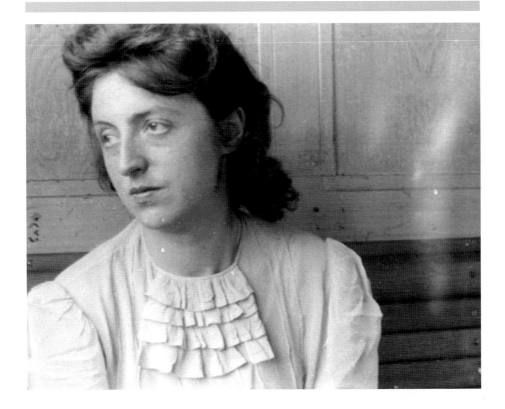

Wednesday, 24 September

On my own today, Foulds having gone off on another of his Berlin trips. Fairly busy in consequence, but finished at 15.00 hrs and did not subsequently have occasion to return to SSQ. Did some work this afternoon and then this evening printed and enlarged some very good negatives sent to me today by Tim. Whilst looking through the *BMJ* tonight came across a notice of my promotion to Flight Lieutenant.

Thursday, 25 September

Even more occupied today, but nothing exciting. Home and worked for about 1½ hours whilst J was away at Guides. Remainder of evening spent reading and listening to a 'trick' play about the Earl of Anglesey's efforts to regain his birthright after his abduction in childhood by his wicked uncle.

Dear Dad   *Thury. 25.ix.47*

Henceforward, we are told, mail to BAOR will travel by surface routes unless prepaid at Air Mail rates – I think the slower method should suffice for the bulk of our correspondence. A 'postal area' scheme has been introduced at the same time and in future the numeral should be added to the address, e.g. BAOR (8).

…One other amendment. I note that the current BMJ announces that 'F/O R. Harrison … to be Flight Lieutenant' – this was the first intimation of the promotion, but I expect it will be confirmed by signal during the next few days.

Received some moe fish food today in your letter of Tuesday … incidentally the fourth anniversary of my meeting Joyce, and an occasion marked by the exchange of suitable small gifts …

Saturday, 27 September

Up at usual time: nothing unusual this morning – rather quiet in fact. Joyce went to Celle today for a Guides meeting, so I prepared my own lunch, did some work and some wireless and then went down to meet her. This evening went with her to see the local schoolchildren do some scenes from *Midsummer Night's Dream* – quite entertaining and with some professional production touches – good grouping and 'business'.

Sunday, 28 September

Rose at 11.00 hrs and then did an hour's work before lunch, and before going to camp to look over the prisoners as usual.

Collected my mail – including Keith Simpson's new 'Forensic Medicine' and spent rest of day working on a radio-chassis.

At about 20.00 hrs Foulds – who returned from Berlin this evening – came down and spent his usual Sunday night with us. To bed at 14.00 hrs after listening to 2nd instalment of 'Gilbert & Sullivan.

Salzbrückerstraße/Obere Ohlinger Straße

Tuesday, 30 September

This afternoon started the 'Admin Course' lectures again with one on hygiene – the better delivered, probably, because of a rest in recent months. Home as usual and did about an hour's work.

Then Skirly came down and the three of us went to see *My Favourite Brunette* – Bob Hope, at his funniest and best, in a pretty lengthy effort. To bed at the late hour – early for the three of us – at 01.30 hrs.

Meanwh[...]
think you will like[...]

work and, with a warm

R
Desi[...]

OCTOBER 1947

Friday, 3 October

Up at 08.00 hrs. Took Denys up to SSQ to park her there. Then collected J and went up to Hamburg in the Volkswagen – since I nominally was on a business trip, trying to recover some blankets missing from the lorry smash last month. Made a short – and, of course, fruitless – visit to the 94th hospital and then went shopping. I bought a good perforator, long scissors and a Gigli saw; later, a useful little photographic rangefinder.

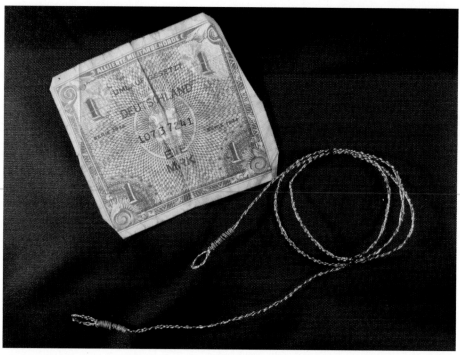

The Gigli saw that Richard bought. It was invented by Italian obstetrician Leonardo Gigli and is a flexible wire (as seen above) used by surgeons for cutting bone. It was mainly used for amputation where the bone needed to be cut smoothly. The saw was occasionally hidden in the clothing of British secret agents during World War II.

Had lunch in a new spot – the 'Four Seasons' beside the Alster. Afterwards concluded our shopping – buying a little picture of an Alpine chalet for 500 Rm and an Air Mail cover for Tim. Home about 18.00 hrs and did an hour's work and then spent the evening mounting the rangefinder on my camera.

Saturday, 4 October

This afternoon attended the Gymkhana of the Riding Club on the Unit; then back home – evening reading and writing.

Dear Dad   Saty. 4.x.47

Nothing spectacular from here – my F/L has been confirmed and I'm just looking round for a bit of braid at the moment. Had a trip with Joyce up to Hamburg yesterday, having a very small item of official business to justify the expedition! Bought a few more instruments for your handsome collection, a few items for the household and the handsome first-day cover for Tim which is enclosed herewith. The price first asked for it suggests it is valuable … must now save up to buy him a blue Cape triangular!

This afternoon has been fairly sunny, so we've been to a local Gymkhana. But the weather generally has been rather chilly of late and we've now started evening fires.

Thanks for all the fish food – no, the denizens of my tank are not so voracious that you need buy another packet just yet. I'm a bit apprehensive about the fate of these chaps as winter approaches – if conditions parallel those here last year, the tank will certainly freeze solid unless it stands on the electric stove!

Sunday, 5 October

Back to winter time today, so I rose at 10.45 hrs feeling very refreshed. Did an hour's work, then spent remainder of morning and afternoon – save for the usual postprandial nap – developing, writing letters and building a wireless receiver.

Walked up to the camp at about 17.00 hrs to see the prisoners. Collected Skirly and returned to our flat for dinner and a listening session to the very fine weekly series on Gilbert & Sullivan.

Monday, 6 October

A most tiring day – plenty of routine work, a big sick parade and this afternoon the initiation of the monthly FFI examinations – 1 case of head lice, 2 of 'crabs' and about 6 each of Scabies and Tinea cruris in 200 men. Found the sight of 200 sets of genitalia very tiring!

Then, at the end of a busy afternoon, had to deliver an address to my biggest audience yet – the whole unit, 1,000 strong. Very disgusted – partly because the G/C was there and partly because I had only vague platitudes to utter – I spoke badly – too fast and with poor pitch.

Good two hours' work tonight, then listened to second half of *Macbeth* on the radio.

Tuesday, 7 October

A much calmer day – passed uneventfully. Very pleased on examining a skin graft over the end of a crushed phalanx, effected by me eight days ago, to find it had taken well.

This evening did a good two hours' work then had a short listening session on the radio ('Mystery Playhouse') and then carried out some enlargements of last weekend's negatives.

Wednesday, 8 October

Foulds went off to Hamburg today – I nevertheless had a not-more-hectic-than-usual morning and had a chance to write a substantial part of a VD report for the PMO.

Home fairly early – 15.00 hrs – after I'd had a haircut. Went out 'shopping' this afternoon with uniformly successful results and debated as to whether or not to buy a rather expensive plate camera I saw.

Came home, put in a good two hours' work this evening, and then ran off a few prints.

Dear Dad   *Wedy. 8.x.47*

I've sent off some parcels to Mill Hill. One – on Saturday last – is a sort of pump cum scent spray gadget for gynaecology and yesterday I sent off XXV in the way of instruments in a box labelled 'Tetanus Toxoid': the same post carried 'Last Days', this latter as a registered parcel. Hope you'll enjoy this – it derived some of its interest for us, of course, because we read it immediately after our return from Berlin. The book is Joyce's, and she wants her people to read it – so can you hang onto the wrapping and send it off again (Daventry) when you and Scottie have finished?

Thanks for the enquiries etc about the insurance – I'll draw up an inventory as you suggest. At the moment things are pretty busy – a big VD drive is on, and apart from this other squadrons are arriving here as other stations close down to economise on manpower. We're well over a thousand strong now … can I claim to have spoken to a larger gathering than you?

The prospects for UK leave are poor – the prices are not quite so prohibitive as I had heard, but J has now got the idea that a short return would make her very nostalgic – she misses the old BBC atmosphere a bit, and has a lot of time on her hands here. She wants me to return to the UK alone, but of course – much though I'd like to have a week or so in Moo Hoo, that's unthinkable. She's a funny girl!!! I'll let you know our eventual decision later, but it can be predicted.

Incidentally, a scheme for visitors (up to 1 month) to BAFO is now aloft. If you and Grace – or Alice (max 2 visitors) would like to stump up the £15 odd in fares, will be happy to put you up – feed you up – and show you how the Occupation forces live.

Thursday, 9 October

More FFIs today – two hundred odd sets of genitalia flicking before our eyes! Otherwise an uninspired day – bought Joyce a negligée and returned home to put in a couple of hours good work.

A narrow Lüneburg street with St Michaeliskirche in the background

Friday, 10 October

For a Friday, today was quiet – finished our last big bunch of FFIs this afternoon and completed the report on Hygiene recently asked for by the PMO.

Dear Dad   *Suny. 12.x.47*

Pleased to hear Tim's specimen arrived safely – because it cost me ninepence in local currency! I note your kind offer on his behalf, but the difficulty is one of supply, not of finance: but I'm keeping my eyes open with him in mind.

Had a note from him today – describing his functions in the Tattoo, in which he leads a very fiery and explosive column in an episode from the Burma campaign. He had sent another negative for my attention. When do I receive this circular letter?

Fine day today – I've been out with Foulds round the local ponds to replenish the plants in my aquarium, and we've had a surprise visit – our first – from J's brother*.

*[Captain Alex Masters, Royal Engineers posted to Germany to conduct the demolition of Belsen]

Wednesday, 15 October

After a long delay – because the ambulance was U/S – Joyce and I went up to Hamburg today in a 15 cwt – nominally so that I could deliver some blankets to the Germans who assisted RAF personnel after the Winsen 'prang'.

Had my usual prowl round the shops and bought a few instruments – notably a very neat little Tracheotomy set in a metal case. Had a good lunch at the Four Seasons (Vier Jahreszeiten). When it came to the time to return though, our lorry didn't materialise and Joyce – who badly wanted to go to the cinema in Lüneburg – was inclined to 'bind'. However, the Padre rolled up in a Volkswagen and, having got her safely en route, I hitch-hiked and arrived about 20 minutes later than she did.

Fould, Joyce and I went to see *Nicholas Nickleby* – good, but not so good as *Great Expectations*, the melodrama being rather thickly smeared in parts.

Dear Dad   *15.x.47 23.00 hrs*

Sorry to hear of Ellis' failure … it seems that he's not cut out for an academic career and I don't know whether to admire or criticise his persistency. Incidentally, Joyce has taken up the traces again and is doing a correspondence course for Inter BSc (Econ.) – she has, of course, already got the necessary Matric. plus a Commercial School Certificate, and has done a year's Economics subsequently. Any question of completing the whole course is impossible to assess as yet – it means another three years work – but it's a welcome aid to passing the rather dull days here and she feels she's getting 'stale', so I've encouraged the scheme.

Friday, 17 October

A wasted day – took sick parade and then met W/C Mattingley and set off with him to 85 Wing HQ at Utersen. Left Lüneburg at about 11.00 hrs and did not arrive – because we did not know the way – until 13.35 hrs. Had an indifferent lunch, then attended the AOC's conference on VD – a dreary business with all the old subject matter on layout of ET rooms, issue of condoms etc – lightened only by an RC padre's diatribe on Immorality, and by the announcement of one MO (F/O Dunn) that he would not disclose any diagnosis to his CO or anyone else – the subject of a long discussion afterwards between him, the SMO and the other doctors. He was, however, quite adamant and one wonders what will be the result of his attitude. I sympathise with it, but cannot believe it is the best from his point of view or – in the long run – the patients'.

Long journey home on a dark, wet road, 18.00–23.00 hrs. Mattingley – a more cheerful and friendly soul than I had thought to date – came to dinner with us and exhibited pictures of his family.

Saturday, 18 October

Had to visit Mrs P, a German wife and listen to a wealth of pathological and gynaecological detail about her possible miscarriage. After lunch went out to find – without conspicuous success – some Lüneburg scenes to photograph.

Sunday, 19 October
Did not rise until about 11.00 hrs, but then put in a good two hours' revision before going out for a stroll round St Michael's Chutch with my Retina. Home for a late lunch after photographing e.g. some cannon balls embedded in a house (below and opposite) – a reputed relic of Napoleon's Army in 1813.

Spent the afternoon and early evening printing some negatives, then up to the camp to collect Foulds. Listened to use usual 'Gilbert & Sullivan' instalment on the wireless and finished the day with a few successful experiments with my 'new' plate camera in the best Victorian style.

Monday, 20 October
Heavy sick parade this morning but – save for the usual families clinic this afternoon – remainder of the day very quiet. Wrote to Tim, sent some instruments off home and then came back to the flat and did about an hour and a half's work. Temperature fell with a bang tonight – a minimal temperature of –4°C was forecast and by midnight the prophecy showed every sign of being justified.

Playing by the steps of St. Michaeliskirche, Lüneburg

Children sitting on the steps of St. Michaeliskirche, Lüneburg

Monday 20 October (continued)

Had a letter from Tim today, describing his part in the set-piece of the Nairobi Tattoo and this – plus his 'circular letter' written on arrival in Africa which has just reached me, provided about ten minutes very entertaining reading. He's in the company of Ugandan askaris who live with their wives in a military formation under conditions which are, by UK standards, to put it mildly, amusing.

Also a letter – perhaps my last – from Patricia who, estranged from her husband (probably through faults on both sides) sails for the States on the 7th of next month.

Tuesday, 21 October

All quiet today. Came home at about 17.00 hrs and did about one and a half hours'
work on my own before going round to join J at Trudie's, where I was regaled with a
rather soggy form of steamed dumpling which made me feel increasingly queasy during
the remainder of the evening. Home at about 22.00 hrs – when Trudie went on night
duty – and then did a little reading before retiring to bed.

Dear Dad   *Tues. 21.x.47*

*I'm pleased to hear all my miscellany of packages arrived safely and trust that by now
you're well away with the 'Last Days'. As for Phillips' samples (for which I never
wrote: ?spontaneous) etc. the family is welcome to utilise what it fancies in return for
the labour of collecting the more abstruse samples. (Incidentally, don't use 'Sterogyl'
which is more potent stuff than it may seem.)*

*Had a session with The Borgias last night, and have a number of other items
earmarked for later in the week – notably another Williams play on Saturday Night
theatre.*

*No more news of my leave – I'm still waiting to hear if my reservation at the rest centre
in Austria has been accepted. Joyce seems definitely set against going home before my
tour expires …*

Friday, 24 October

Pretty busy with the usual trivial round – the more so as Foulds went off this afternoon
to attend a lecture by an Army Colonel – the reports of which suggest that masturbation
was advocated as the cure for the commonest of ills prevailing in BAFO.

I gave my usual harangue to the NCO's course on hygiene.

Tonight Kirkland and Foulds accompanied J to a local Symphony Concert whilst I
stayed at home and did some work and developed a film. Usual conversation until the
wee sma' hours on their return and so to bed.

Directing traffic outside the Rathaus, Lüneburg

Saturday, 25 October

Did not rise until 11.30 hrs with the result that the day seemed a very short one. However, did an hour's Anatomy, printed some enlargements and visited the camp to see the prisoners.

This evening Kirkland and Foulds came to dinner, and together we heard the sixth and last of the very fine programmes dealing with the partnership of Gilbert & Sullivan.

Dear Dad   *Suny. 26.x.47*

Beginning to get ready for the winter and everyone glad to have the heat on at last. Next week is likely to be a fully occupied one – including as it does a dining-in night, Mess dance and the local boxing tournament at which Max Schmeling [a famous German heavyweight boxer who had served in the German Army] is booked to give a demonstration. RH has a ringside seat as official MO … Heard 'Trespass' last night and tonight the MO and the Dental Officer are dining here to hear the end of Gilbert & Sullivan. Goodness only knows what we will do on Sunday evenings in future!

An orderly reading at SSQ, Lüneburg

Monday, 27 October

Slept on the divan, which I was sharing with J until 05.00 hrs when I was telephoned from CRS – two RAF men had been admitted after a Volkswagen crash in which a third was killed. They were from a Hamburg unit.

Took the ambulance down and collected two sergeants – one with an ugly scalp wound and one cut about the face.

Back to bed at 07.00 hrs for an hour's nap, after effecting preliminary dressings. Later, after a lengthy sick parade – Hunterian chancres [syphilis] – Foulds and I sutured the casualties and generally had a busy day.

Listened to the radio tonight – play on family life by Van Druten. To bed, very tired.

Tuesday, 28 October

Felt very tired tonight and in consequence slept soundly until 08.50 hrs! Arrived at SSQ about 09.20 hrs – a light day in comparison with yesterday, followed. Gave my usual hygiene lecture – which is becoming very much of a recitation – followed.

Home at 18.00 hrs. Did about an hour's work and we had an early dinner because Monica and her sister came round afterwards. Joyce occupied by her first lesson in the BSc. Econ. course.

Wednesday, 29 October
Suffering from a mild coryza [common cold] today – finished work at 13.00 hrs and came home. Did a fairly intensive three hours' work this afternoon and went to the YMCA for tea. Had intended to spend part of the evening in the darkroom, but felt indisposed for it and sat down and had a quiet read instead. To bed early (23.10 hrs) with a cup of coffee, hot water bottle and a couple of tablets of Captain Dover's favourite remedy.

Dear Dad   *Wedy. 29.x.47*

I note your remarks re a holiday in Germany and must say that I haven't to date given the matter much thought because I didn't think you'd want to make a long, and not inexpensive, trip. However, I've now collected the necessary forms and information. Briefly:

1. *Only 75 visitors in all Germany at any one time. The demand for permits though, is at present slight and you can probably be sure of a place.*
2. *Only 2 for a given family. Will Grace come with you? Or Alice? (Tim writes 'How about fixing Jean and I up for the demob leave!')*
3. *You must have a valid passport, which will be issued with a Military Entry Permit by Air Ministry for periods of up to 4 weeks. I think to make the trip worthwhile you should come for 2–3 weeks at least.*
4. *Pay your own fare – about £15 return each. Rations, transport, etc. over here is through ordinary service channels, debited against me.*
5. *I must give dates and names on the forms. I suggest that you do not come before the end of February because travelling is so appalling up till then that you'd see little of Germany. After that date I could probably fix up a Berlin excursion etc.*

Joyce with some local children in Lüneburg

Thursday, 30 October

Nothing much in SSQ today – removed a wart from a man's hand this afternoon; came home at 17.15 hrs and had a good two and a half hours on the books whilst J was at the Guides. After dinner printed some of Tim's negatives and then read a chapter of Novak's *Pathology* which I received today. So to bed.

Friday, 31 October

Nothing epoch-making today – J went out with Trudie tonight to the local theatre, so I stayed in, wrote a letter and did some revision.

Had a letter today from Bob Cocks – he married Maureen O'Donnell yesterday. Has been commissioned in the RAMC and expects to come out to Germany in a week or so. Joyce very pleased about it all. I'm glad to think – as J pointed out – that this ties the little clique together once more – even Ellis is involved, as he was best man.

Lüneburg Airfield Main Gate

Lüneburg Flying Control interior

Meanwhile I think you will like work and, with a warm

R. Dest

NOVEMBER 1947

NOVEMBER 1947

Saturday, 1 November
Morning principally occupied with a rather unusual case – F/O Foulds had been called at about 07.00 hrs to see a baby girl about 6/12 which, sleeping with another child, was found by its parents to be lying underneath the sheet in a cyanosed condition. He gave it some brandy and left some Sulphathiazole for it: when he described its condition to me I suggested that it be transferred to the 94th BMH. But whilst we were considering this, a phone message requested us to go down, and the child was, when we arrived, blue and quite dead. We went through the usual drill, but of course made no impression on it. I rather think the child died of fulminating pneumonia and feel rather inclined to dismiss the blanket incident as a cause of death.

This afternoon had a stroll round the town and read and did odd jobs until the time to prepare for this evening's dance came round.

To the dance tonight – big crowd, but I (and many others) spent most of the time waiting for the buffet to open. When it did I had plenty of trifle, pork and duck, but concluded I felt rather sorry that the feed had been rather late in the day and that I could have done myself more justice in two or three attacks at hourly intervals!

Had one casualty during the evening – F/Lt Muller burnt his chin trying to drink a burning liqueur. When I'd dressed this, spent three quarters of an hour at the Sergeants' Mess dance. Home at about 03.00 hrs.

Sunday, 2 November
Did not rise until 12.00 hrs: then had some fish at a late lunch and, to the poor state of preservation of this, rather than to any of last night's indulgences, attribute the fact that at 22.00 hrs, in the presence of Foulds and Kirkland, who came down for the evening to the flat, I had to retire. I ended the day by being violently and repeatedly sick and having diarrhoea. Really felt *in extremis*. My second similar episode ascribed to 'bad fish' in recent months.

Monday, 3 November

Rose from the bed of sickness at 06.30 hrs to go out on an errand of mercy. Mrs C – a still doubtful pregnancy at 3/12 – had started to bleed heavily p.v. Could not, fishing through the sanguinous mass in the bathroom, find any foetal products. Gave her Morphine and returned to bed. In view of my nausea, remained there till noon.

However, after breakfast cum lunch, went to the aerodrome and did a full aftenoon's work.

Spitfire PM156 in the snow at the aerodrome, Lüneburg

Lüneburg – Spifire PR X1

The final variant of the Spitfire family to be built specifically as a specialist photo-recce aircraft, optimised for flight at high speed and high altitude, was the Spitfire PR. The Spitfire PR Mk XI was completely unarmed, carrying additional fuel in place of the guns of the fighter versions giving it an operational range of 1,500 miles. The Rolls-Royce Griffon, 37-litre, V-12 engine, producing over 2,000 horsepower.

Dear Dad   Mony. 3.xi.47

My usual note of the weekend herewith – the chief item of interest being the big dance at the Mess from 20.00–03.00 hrs on Saturday night – big crowd there. Alice would have enjoyed the late hours and the cabaret. There was also a mighty fine buffet, with a pig's head (boar, I mean) roasted whole, lashings of duck, pork, salads and trifles etc. However, of all these things I am able to write only with some considerable willpower, because on Sunday morning, after lying in bed until a suitable hour, I rose and ate a piece of fish that wasn't all it might have been – with the result that I'm just beginning to pull round tonight from a very debilitating dose of 'bellywaache'!

Had your note of the 28th today, in which you acknowledge receipt of a parcel of tools. I cannot understand your remarks about the range-finder – the package in question contained:

Four surgical instruments:
- *1 mouth gag (a big pair of forceps with a movable ratchet).*
- *1 pr PM rib shears (cutting blades, like secateurs).*
- *1 pr Spencer Wells with needle pointed blades.*
- *1 needle holder – long thin beak-like with a small pair of pliers.*

Plus 1 lens hood – a very obvious shade of metal, in black, and the range-finder itself – made in wood and metal, about 2 in long, labelled PHOTOMETER in big letters and this shape:

If nothing corresponding to this description is there, I can only presume some artful b ——— has quietly unpacked the parcel en route. I take it there's no Custom's note?

Quite fit now, Dick

Wednesday, 5 November
This afternoon worked at home. Joyce went out to a concert this evening – I, Foulds and the Dental Officer, went to the cinema and saw a rather complicated 'thriller' *The High Window*.

This morning S/Ldr Tonkinson came down to lecture on VD, bringing with him a German woman (whom I photographed) having a syphilitic gumma of the face to show the men. One reaction to the exhibition of this case was overheard by an orderly of mine, who subsequently said, 'The old woman's face was bloody awful – but I could have shagged that nurse with her!'

Thursday, 6 November
Quiet day – did some work this evening and then printed some photographs.

The Officers' Mess set up for dinner

Friday, 7 November

Foulds went off for a weekend this morning and I was left to do the routine work of the station – a job which has become progressively more onerous with the steady increase in our strength during recent months. We now have over 1,000 men here, with about a 100 families – a different state of affairs from that prevailing at the end of the winter, when we had about 600 men and 50–60 families.

Dear Dad   *Friday. 7.xi.47*

All quiet here – working hard all day at hundreds of useless jobs, whence the sensation of being 'browned off' which you remark on in your letter. I'll be glad to walk the wards of a hospital again and to see somebody really ill that I can really treat – that's to say if any respectable hospital will still accept me!

Still waiting to hear about my leave – I've been granted the first fortnight in December (my opposite number is getting married in the UK in the second!) and, as I think I told you, I've applied for accommodation at a winter sports centre – Ehrwald – in North Austria. But the place is in the French Zone and I'm still waiting to hear whether I can go. I'd still rather come back to No 5, but Joyce is very upset at the idea of a fleeting glimpse of the Old Country before she can go back for good.

One request – can you pack up that uniform of mine at your leisure and send it off? Having bought it I might as well wear it, since my second-hand one is beginning to look rather poor at the Mess functions, though quite suitable for all other occasions.

Yours aye,
Dick

P.S.   The big boxing match has been postponed – is taking place before a big audience in one of our hangars on the 14th.

P.P.S. Just seen the Radio Times – promises to be a good week on the air next week.

Saturday, 8 November

Heavy sick parade on my own – did not finish it until about 11.00 hrs, when a whole series of other jobs followed in its wake.

Home at 13.15 hrs and had a smoke and sit down after lunch; from this I was roused by a call to stitch up three members of a visiting Rugger team whose transport had become involved with a tree. When I returned from this task, it was too late to go for my usual Saturday afternoon stroll, so I did odd jobs until dinner. Then a short spell in the darkroom and listened to the radio – the Festival of Remembrance and a very pointless Saturday Night Theatre by Compton Mackenzie.

Sunday, 9 November

Very quiet day – worked all morning and this evening Kirkland came down to spend the evening with us – together we listened to a review of the History of Broadcasting – the first of a week's programmes commemorating the 25th Jubilee of the BBC.

A Luftwaffe gravy spoon 'liberated' by RH from the Mess

Tuesday, 11 November

Did a pretty full day's work – including the interviewing of a homosexual corporal, charged with writing an indecent letter. He admitted to indulging in homosexual practices – always in the 'female' role – ever since the age of 14 when, as a newspaper boy, he was importuned by a solicitor. Since then he has lived with men for periods up to 4/12, and returns to one particular individual at every leave.

During the day, however, and especially towards its end, I began to feel a cold overtaking me. When I arrived home I felt so groggy that I retired straight to bed, remaining however, sufficiently *compos mentis* to listen to a programme on the workings of the BBC. Then took a couple of Dover's powders and so to sleep.

Wednesday, 12 November

Arose about 08.30 hrs and considered the prospects of going to work – but I felt so dizzy and sick (the results, no doubt, of my idiosyncrasy to opiates) that I remained in bed and slept intermittently all morning. By the afternoon all the symptoms of nasal catarrh etc. had disappeared but I was left with a vague malaise and a tendency to perspire and feel weak on any exertion. So remained where I was all day, reading and writing a few letters and sympathising with such of my patients who had the misfortune to spend long periods abed. Most of the evening spent listening to the radio and renewing an acquaintance with A. J. Alan who – by written and spoken word – never fails to please me.

Thursday, 13 November

Felt quite fit today and went into work as usual only a few minutes late – had a pretty quiet day, came home at the customary time and spent two hours on the books and the rest of the evening reading and listening to the wireless – a Jubilee Edition of *ITMA* [*It's That Man Again* a comedy radio programme] and a play about a cursed cottage in Shropshire.

Friday, 14 November

Normal working day – came home at 17.40 hrs and left again at 20.10 hrs to act as MO for the Boxing Contest held in a hangar on the 'drome. A dozen odd bouts fought between the RAF and the Army with perhaps more vigour than technique – but very

Armistice Day Parade, Lüneburg

enjoyable. One bod knocked through the ropes onto the floor. Max Schmeling, ex-heavyweight champion, gave four rather tame exhibition bouts. Home at 23.15 hrs and, after a very short read, to bed.

Saturday, 15 November
Joyce and I went out for a walk this afternoon – tonight we listened to Frank Collier – *The Winslow Boy*.

Sunday, 16 November
Did a good couple of hours work, then very little else – apart from completing the photo printing box for the dark room – for the rest of the day. Tonight Foulds and the DO came down to listen to the wireless and J and I slept in discomfort on our narrow divan.

Air Marshal Tedder's DC3 outside the hangar at Lüneburg aerodrome

Monday, 17 November

Up at 05.00 hrs to turn the fish tank heater on. Rose at 08.15 hrs and so to SSQ. A very quiet day, but relaxation impossible because we awaited the visit of Air-Marshal Wigglesworth, AOC in C of BAFO. When he did arrive, it was at a time when SSQ had decided he wasn't coming and we were all having tea. However, he was a more friendly type than Flynn, the rather sober AOC 85 Wing.

Home at 18.00 hrs – two good hours' work and read Novak on Ovarian Tumours for an hour.

Today was pretty cold – we saw our first snowflakes, in considerable numbers, this morning.

RH with Alex Masters, Joyce's brother, a Captain in the Royal Engineers at Victory Hill, Lüneburg Heath

Tuesday, 18 November
Fairly busy day – tried the experiment of lunching at home. This afternoon watched an unsuccessful attempt at anaesthetising a very heavily-built Irishman, in a dental chair, with Pentothal – it failed because no adequate airway could be maintained and because an inflammatory swelling restricted the extent to which we could open his mouth.

Dear Dad   *Tuesy. 18.xi.47*

Pleased to see two notes from you on Monday and to hear that my food parcel had reached you – in view of the admittedly attractive nature of some of its contents, I felt that it might well 'disappear' en route. I hope to get one more off early in December. Meanwhile there's another proposal for you – Joyce thinks that Stilton and Rochefort cheeses may now be available at home on points, whereas out here we get only a very poor processed variety. If Grace would like to use some of your points to buy a bit of funny cheese – not the liquid Camembert though – will send you in return a Xmas pudding or tin of meat pie or tinned turkey or some such commodity.

The weekend has been disturbed by one other event(s). We've had a high mortality amongst the fish, with the onset of winter, but on Sunday on looking at the tank I saw one of our survivors had been delivered of 17 young fish! (Delivered is correct – these tropical fish are, in several cases, viviparous). All are doing well so far.

Wednesday, 19 November
Today we planned to spend doing some Xmas shopping in Hamburg. Joyce and I got away to an early start, in the ambulance – but on arrival in the City found to our horror that today is celebrated as a public holiday for Advent! Subsequent to this, we felt a bit depressed – we strolled round the (British) establishments that were open and bought J some slippers for her Xmas present.

Lunched in the 'Four Seasons', had another stroll and met the ambulance at 15.45 hrs. So home, where I had to see a patient whom Foulds considered – probably correctly – to

The Docks, Stade

have acute nephritis following tonsillitis. Sent him off to the 94th and then J and I went to the cinema. Saw *The Egg and I* – Claudette Colbert in a comedy about the struggles of a chicken farmer.

Thursday, 20 November

Pretty busy, but uneventful, day at SSQ. Came, for lunch, back to the flat and heard most of the commentary on Princess Elizabeth's wedding. J always feels very sentimental about weddings – perhaps I do too, because I found myself envying him all the excitement. Not that the big day was the less happy or less strenuous for me – I found myself still remembering it better than I remember, perhaps, any other 12 hours of my life.

Home tonight and did a fair evening's work whilst J was out with the Guides. Worried about Denys who is having a peculiar intermittent convulsion movement of her jaws, for which I gave her some Sodium Bromide. A rather depressing, murky day.

Friday, 21 November

Got away to a rather late start for Hamburg – this time leaving J behind – and arrived there about 11.40 hrs in a mild drizzle. Visited my usual surgical instrument shops without acquiring anything remarkable, but did get a useful Spinal Manometer and a Sphygmomanometer. Then bought a couple of Xmas presents and, gaining access to the British bookshop before it was officially open, bought a couple of books for J.

Home at 18.15 hrs to find Denys in poor condition – a German vet says she has cerebral distemper. Gave her injections of Nambutal to control the convulsive movements of the jaws from which she is suffering, but had to go on rather an empirical dosage. She seems to take even gms 1/2 without much apparent effect.

Dining-in night at the Mess – more attractive function than last time, but I left at a comparatively early hour and came home.

Dear Dad   *Saty. 22.xi.47*

Today had some very bad news – my colleague, Foulds, is being posted to Stade. The MO from there – the most incompetent detestable man I've met for a long time – is coming here ... to be under my supervision whilst he awaits a singularly well deserved court martial for flogging RAF stores! I'm very sorry because Foulds, Joyce and I were all great pals: when X finally gets his deserts, I trust Foulds will get back.

Finally, Denys has developed cerebral distemper. The German vet doesn't seem to have much of a grip on the situation, and Joyce is breaking her heart whilst I try to discover the appropriate dosage of various drugs by a process of trial and error. However, the dog can't be terribly ill and I have high hopes of her recovery. My seventeen baby fish are doing well.

Yours aye,
Dick

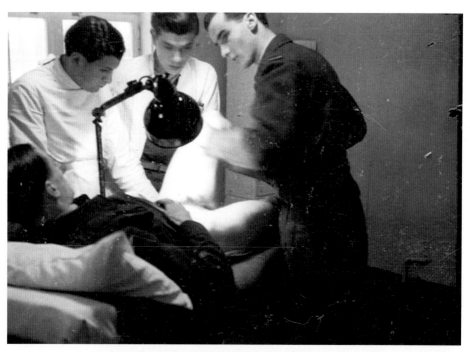

A medical examination at SSQ and below RH smoking his pipe at SSQ

Saturday, 22 November

Today I rose late because the unit had a half holiday following the AOC's inspection. As I was having my shave, Foulds arrived with the unwelcome news that he was being posted. It subsequently transpired that F/Lt X was awaiting court martial for selling service stores – Penicillin as I suspect – from RAF Uttersen. [This was later proved to be erroneous, but a similar incident had been the subject of the film *The Third Man*.] He is – to my regret – to come to Lüneburg so that I can keep an eye on him. Suicide seems to be in S/L Tonkinson's mind who described him on the phone as a 'melancholy little sod'.

Went up to SSQ after this depressing news, and came home about 14.00 hrs. Tonight Foulds and Kirkland came down for a last evening together – we went to see a film of the early days of Air Mails, *Blaze of Noon*. Then sat up until 03.00 hrs, smoking, drinking coffee and listening to a good play – *The Guinea Pig* – dealing with the Public School system.

Sunday, 23 November

Rose at 10.30 hrs and went up to SSQ to see the odd 'special side' etc. Home and spent the rest of the day working and reading.

Dear Dad   *Suny. 23.xi.47*

Thanks for the pamphlet on the Surgical Encyclopaedia – edited, as you no doubt noticed – by my old chief Paterson Ross. I've written for further details … I could probably raise (if the volumes seem worth it) £3 per number, at intervals of six to twelve months. But if they publish all the volumes in a rush it would be a nasty strain!

The Xmas mail starts herewith – the enclosed stamps, and any you receive before the 25th on Tim's Xmas present, should be collected in a separate envelope lest there be any doubt I have got him one! In addition I am tomorrow posting a small pocket chess set, better than, and to replace, the one that got lost. Alice's present also takes to the road tomorrow.

Monday, 24 November

Busy morning, working on my own – Sick Parade went on till 10.50 hrs but this afternoon was easier. Had to return home at lunchtime, as J was worried about Denys – who, however, was quite fit when I saw her. Took her down to the vets for a second injection of antiserum, and had a job getting away from the talkative, pleasant old chap.

Tonight listened – after about 2½ hours – to Somerset Maugham's play about a fugitive from a 'crime passionel' – *The Narrow Corner*.

Tuesday, 25 November

Rather quieter today – still no signs of X. The day's biggest surprise has been the sudden news of the posting of Cpl Baxter and – to his great astonishment – Sgt Williams! Much telephoning on his part to try to correct this unprecedented interference of Air Ministry with his peaceful existence in Lüneburg.

Dear Dad   *Tuesy. 25.xi.47*

Absolute chaos at 151 R.U. – four hundred Senior NCOs are being repatriated (cutting down forces in BAOR?) and work at a standstill in consequence. Worst of all – my sergeant, the pillar of SSQ AND my senior corporal – have just received their marching orders too! And little RH still on his own, with no signs of this delinquent MO as yet!

Had a note from Tim today – but nothing exciting to report. He says he is fed up of receiving pictures of the Old Crane of Locomotive Fame, but says you have a couple of interesting pictures of the Tattoo. I would be glad to see them if they are of convenient dimensions.

Well, cheerio for now – hope to see a note from you again soon (however vague!) Glad you heard 'The Guinea Pig' and wonder if you heard 'The Narrow Corner' last night.

Wednesday, 26 November
Telephone at 03.10 hrs – had to go up to the sick quarters to see a case of appendicitis –
a man previously sent up for an operation who, when his symptoms improved, declined
treatment in order to go on leave. Put him to bed and sent him up at 09.30 hrs.

Quiet day – Foulds came back for a few hours to clear up a few odds and ends at 151.
Joyce and I had a stroll in town and tea in the YMCA and then did three hours work
apiece. So to bed.

Am Stintmarkt, Lüneburg

Thursday, 27 November
Only notable event today was F/Lt X's arrival – he is now a very much quieter and rather
paler individual, and I have no doubt that the impending court martial is weighing
heavily upon him. Not so much, however, as to prevent him being very keen to get off
to spend this weekend in Hamburg.

Bit worried about Denys – she kept us awake last night with a peculiar repetitive whimper whenever she dropped off to sleep, making me wonder whether some encephalitic process has involved the 'speech' centre. Today she has a slight weakness (or tenderness?) of the rear limbs, but has slept comfortably on 3/4 gm of Nembutal and when she wakes up seems lively enough.

Friday, 28 November
Today came home for lunch and to take Denys to the vet – she negotiated the journey happily enough under own steam, but she is still very lackadaisical and given to these terrible yelping attacks.

This afternoon Joyce brought her up to the P61 and we bought about 30 shillings' worth of tinned food to send home to the Masters and the Harrisons.

Tonight J and I had what at one stage threatened to be a major disagreement, because I'd utilised the Guest Scheme to bring Dad and Grace out in place of her people … one of the proverbial rows about in-laws and as such our first on record. Still, I felt J had sacrificed her people's claim by declining to go home on leave … and Dad has had fewer holidays and seen less of the world than Mr Masters … I wish the scheme wasn't restricted to only two guests, though whether anything at all will ever come of it seems problematical.

Dear Dad   *Friy. 28.xi.47*

All quiet this end – the chief focus of interest being Denys' illness, which is not running too smoothly – she has periods when she looks virtually immobilised and others when she seems not far removed from normal. Joyce is turning rapidly grey, because she's devoted to the little dog; therapy to date has included Nembutal, Bromide, Calomel, Phenobarbital and a diet of gin and raw eggs. In spite of this intensive treatment, plus the serum of doubtful validity contributed by the local vet, my prognosis grows steadily gloomier. Had a bit of snow here this morning – it settled, but not for long. I trust that now the stuff is piling up at our holiday resort in the Tyrrol.

Above: Inside the Station Sick Quarters
Below: RH's bedroom within the Station Sick Quarters

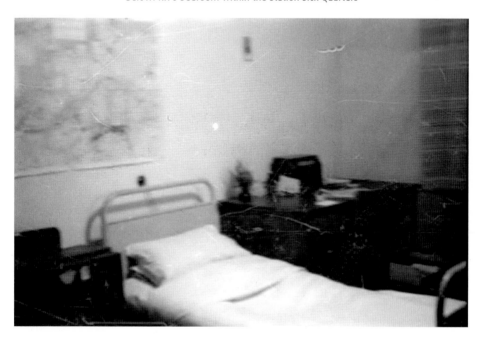

Above: Lüneburg Airfield in the snow
Below: Three Spitfires

Saturday, 29 November
This afternoon devoted to the Colliers who attended en masse for tea. The DO came tonight, and we listened to Bridie's *Mr Bolfry* – the evening being marred by Denys' continued symptoms, and interrupted by the arrival, for my examination, of a man with what looked like early lobar pneumonia.

Sunday, 30 November
Did not rise until 11.00 hrs, then had a late breakfast and went up to the aerodrome with Mickey.

Joyce very distressed because Denys was obviously so much weaker today – we cancelled an appointment to have tea at Trudie's, but later in the evening she came round to see us and to arrange J's German 'Advent Wreath' (see below) – an evergreen circlet bearing four candles, one being lit for every Sunday between now and Xmas.

I spent the evening listening to most of Noël Coward's two-hour *Cavalcade* and recalling memories of seeing it on a wet afternoon in a cinema whilst on a seaside holiday. Then listened to a true story of an RAF officer in Buchenwald. But Denys' illness made the day generally a dreary one and I found myself hoping that the strain of waiting would soon be ended by her demise, for I can hold out little hope of her recovery!

think you will like

work and, with a warm

DECEMBER 1947

DECEMBER 1947

Monday, 1 December

One of those queer disappointing days – an error in my watch resulted in our rising late. At lunchtime Denys' condition was so much better that one could toy with hopes of her recovery. But during the afternoon she apparently howled so much that Joyce was near breaking point when I came home. Furthermore, Denys looked quite paretic and in a poor way. Still feeling that I might have waited a little longer and have tried a little harder, I nevertheless wrapped her up in the old blanket she's had since a pup, and took her down to the German vet. He was emphatic about the nonexistence of the possibility of her recovery, and after I'd given her some intraperitoneal Nembutal – a form of anaesthesia which intrigued him immensely – he gave her intrapulmonary KCV. Home, terribly dejected and took J to the cinema to see the film of the Royal Wedding.

We were both very fond of our little dog – all tonight a lump has shot into my throat whenever I think of her. Not particularly intelligent, she was so human in some of her ways – the manner in which she lay down in our bed, or in Joyce's arms – she seems at this moment to have cost me more sorrow than even old Jock who grew up with us all ever so many years ago. Most of all I mourn that she'd never known all the things which must be Doggy Delights – like a rat, or a plunge in the sea or a race through open fields – but spent all her days in our tiny flat. But anyhow, even there, she was never allowed to feel unhappy for a moment. *Requiesceat in pace.*

Tuesday, 2 December

No real work on my part today – organised the last details of my leave and hung about the court martial room waiting to give evidence and eventually making a brief appearance to make a formal, unquestioned statement about Corporal Curtis' death in a lorry smash on 14 September last. (The driver of the lorry is accused of manslaughter.) Received F/O Leyland, my relief, tonight and came home to read, pack and eventually retire to bed about 02.30 hrs.

Dear Dad   *Tuesy. 2.xii.47*

This is just a brief note before the start of my leave – we're going to have a couple of days in Hamburg, returning on Friday night – when I'll write again. Then on Sunday we set off on our twenty-hour train journey into the Tyrol – and lose contact with civilisation and the mails until about the 18th.

The beginning of the holiday has been marred by tragedy – after a long fight for Denys, during which she bore all my administrations with remarkable tolerance, it became apparent yesterday that a severe degree of paralysis was developing. Furthermore, Joyce had had little or no sleep for three or four nights. So, with very real regret, I gave our little dog a small dose of a suitable anaesthetic and took her down to the vets for some cyanide. The flat seems terrible without her – I suppose a small place like ours isn't the best place to rear a dog, but it has the effect of making it very much a part of the family – she invariably slept on our feet in bed and expected her meals to be put down on the floor at the same time as ours was laid. Even a trip to the cinema to see the Royal Wedding couldn't keep a lump from our throats the rest of the day.

Today I had to appear at the court martial (driver of the lorry that overturned) – but mine was formal evidence of death and I was only detained a few minutes.

Wednesday, 3 December

Up at 08.00 hrs and set about collecting our luggage and shutting up the house, completing these jobs just in time to catch the ambulance at 09.45 hrs. Arrived in Hamburg, at The Four Seasons, on the bank of the Alster, at 11.20 hrs. Having found our room and deposited the bags, went out and had a cup of tea before I did my usual rapid tour of the surgical instrument shops and a second, more leisurely one, of other shops in search of Xmas presents. After lunch continued our researches and paid a visit to the British book shop, where I purchased a volume for Grace.

At 16.30 hrs Skirly met us by arrangement at the hotel – we had tea and then continued the shopping, mostly for his benefit until it was time for dinner – to which he treated us. We went to 'a mystery?' film about adolescent American youth (Edward G Robinson in *The Red House*), had a quick coffee and saw Skirly off back to Stade at 23.10 hrs – back for more coffee and to bed just after midnight. A damp, drizzly day which we all thoroughly enjoyed.

Thursday, 4 December

Rose at 09.00 hrs and had a leisurely breakfast – then J and I divided forces and went on our respective shopping expeditions, though I bought little save a drying press for photographers and an ophthalmoscope for Foulds.

Back for lunch, when we made a meal – capped by liquors – of such dimensions as to incapacitate us for most of the afternoon, so that, save for another brief stroll round the shops, we did little save sit in the hotel and read or talk for the remainder of the day. To bed – distended with this lunch and with a very similar dinner, at 23.30 hrs.

Friday, 5 December

A slightly more marked tardiness in getting up today resulted in our having a cold breakfast. Then we packed and strolled round the shops, but by now most of our purchases had been made and the walk was a desultory one. Back for lunch, and afterwards went back to Lüneburg by ambulance – and, on arrival, spent a steady two hours packing up our few gifts and addressing our Xmas cards. To bed well after midnight.

Hamburg Rathaus (Town Hall)

Saturday, 6 December

Went up to SSQ this morning and collected movement orders etc. for tomorrow. This afternoon J was running a series of stalls organised by the Girl Guides for a Xmas charity – a dozen odd girls came to lunch, so I cooked my own. Remainder of day spent reading and listening half-heartedly to a radio play by Dodie Smith.

Sunday, 7 December

Up at 09.00 hrs and completed the packing. Inevitably we left the flat about ten minutes before the train was due and arrived at the station as it came in. J in her usual fluster and quite unable to relinquish possession of the house unless it was a good deal tidier than it usually is when we are in occupation.

Uneventful journey to Hannover, 12.15–14.30 hrs approx. Then cups of tea and cream cakes in the Red Shield canteen – the one bright spot in what is otherwise, I think, the dreariest spot I know. The Ehrwald train arrived to time at 16.23 hrs and left about half an hour later – Joyce and I shared a compartment with a jovial but loquacious Salvation Army man and a couple from a NAAFI store. Might have had worse travelling companions, and a worse dinner than that we ate later on – though this latter was a scanty meal compared with our repasts of the past few days.

Then, with much reorganisation of the seating arrangements, settled down for the night. Joyce and I on one seat, the couple on the other and the Salvation Army man on seatbacks on the floor. Usual fitful slumbers, but had more sleep than I anticipated – I'm getting good in trains! – and the compartment was, thank God, at a fairly comfortable temperature.

Monday, 8 December

We must have been fairly comfortable for it was with some reluctance the occupants of the compartment roused themselves at about 08.30 hrs. We all had a wash in cold water in the lavatory and watched with interest the gradual increasing mountainous nature of the terrain we were crossing and noted the gradual increase in the depth of snow upon it.

Arrived at Ehrwald, by way of Garmisch, at about 10.30 hrs and detrained into awaiting

Hotel Buchenhain, Ehrwald

3-ton TCVs. We were taken over a rather dicey snow-covered track to a point within walking distance of our hotel – Hotel Buchenhain. A small, spotlessly clean, very sparsely furnished chalet-style building. Our bedroom looks out into a basin formed by great rugged peaks in which the village itself lies. Behind us is The Zugspitze, the highest peak of all.

After a simple lunch went out to borrow our ski equipment and were initiated into the surprisingly complicated business of ski fitting and waxing. By dinner time we felt so tired that we retired immediately to bed and were soon asleep.

Dear Dad   *Mony. 8.xii.47*

Arrived safely back in Lüneburg from Hamburg after a short but luxurious stay, during which we were frequently incapacitated for long periods as a result of various gastronomic excesses.

Upon our return I was happy to find your Camembert 'sample' awaiting us – in a few minutes we are to settle down to a serious attack upon it. Meanwhile, it appears to be in excellent condition.

Will write from Ehrwald when the BAOR train runs back into Germany – about seven days hence – and again immediately I get home.

Tuesday, 9 December

Up early and had a new-laid egg and porridge for breakfast. Spent the morning learning how to carry and walk in skis. How to walk uphill and across slopes, to turn round and – most important of all – how to stand up after falling over. Thoroughly fatigued after two hours and glad of a cup of coffee. After lunch, in a light snow storm, descended gentle slopes and – with less success – tried gliding across slopes. Made less progress this afternoon than this morning – poor J easily the worst pupil in the class, tending to fall backwards after a few yards and to traverse great distances lying on her skis, but, withal, showing great cheerfulness and perseverance.

Tonight, with my wrists aching badly from the alpenstocks, but less tired than last night – out for a short sit in the NAAFI and back to bed about 23.00 hrs. Greyish day with the mountain tops shrouded in thick cloud. Surprisingly hot skiing, and had to take off some of my clothes at lunch time.

Wednesday, 10 December

Very much more confident today on the skis and Joyce coming on very well indeed – no really hard falls today, though the snow is now more tightly packed and is fast acquiring a well-nigh glossy surface, making uphill trekking very hard work. Spent all day on the braking manoeuvre called 'The Snow Plough'.

Joyce on her bottom once again

Luki instructing the art of 'The Snow Plough.
Below 'Husky' Dick and far right Joyce mastering the art of her skis

This evening went down to a dance at the NAAFI – principally to have a snack. Our meals here are rather simple but – save for the sweets – adequate, and the breakfast of fresh egg and bacon and porridge is very good indeed. The surrounding peaks with their snow caps looked very attractive indeed today – hope they'll come out well in some of my pictures.

Thursday, 11 December

More snow overnight – Joyce and I put in a full day skiing – more of the 'Snow Plough' with a constant accompaniment of 'Bend of the Knees', 'Parallel', 'Bend the Knees' from Luki. Very satisfactory progress on the part of both Joyce and I – we concluded the day's tuition with some gentle glides over slopes which we enjoyed.

Day finished on an unexpected and exciting note, working out with Mr Young – a Red Cross worker with whom we fell in on the train coming down – details for a trip tomorrow to the Brenner Pass via Innsbruck – a quite irregular expedition privately organised on a basis of cigarettes. Borrowed an alarm clock, set it for 07.15 hrs and so to bed.

Friday, 12 December

A really memorable day – up at 07.30 hrs and had an early breakfast. An hour later Joyce, I, Young (a BRCS worker) and five ATS girls boarded a tiny little motor bus and set out for Innsbruck, about 40 km away. We drove through the Fern Pass – a fine gorge, the beauty of which was somewhat impaired for me by the undoubtedly treacherous nature of the snowy road through it. The driver, however, seemed very capable and we arrived safely at 11.00 hrs. Innsbruck – under French Occupation – is an airy, pleasant town surprisingly backed by snowy mountains.

Innsbruck with its flags flying to celebrate the return of Austrian PoWs from the Soviet Union

From Innsbruck we caught the Milan Express at 12.10 hrs – without the benefit of tickets, movement orders etc. I gave the conductor four cigarettes and found him obviously incapable of coping with our unauthorised presence. Left the train at a little mountain village – Steinach – and there consumed our sandwiches and purchased coffee all round for ten cigarettes. About 14.00 hrs we caught a slow train and travelled up the Brenner Pass, via Greis-Brenner. Descended at the little frontier village of Brennersee and from their walked for five minutes to the Italian frontier. The Pass is remarkable enough, but not, I think, more impressive than the more rugged country of the Pyrenées–Orientes near Prades and Mont-Louis and Thermes de Bains-les-Bains. Came back in a crowded, slow train to Innsbruck, where the same bus awaited us – a slow drive back, but less nerve-wracking since in the dark we couldn't see the edges of the road – or the lack of them! Arrived home ravenously hungry and closed the day in the NAAFI, with thanks that Britain, as an island, was spared all this 'frontier business'.

RH and Joyce at the Brenner Pass and below somewhere close to the Italian frontier

Pension Buchenhain

Ehrwald

Tyrol

Austria

12.xii.47

Dear Dad

Arrived at Ehrwald in a heavy snowstorm about 10.30 hrs and detrained into TCV lorries – about 130 odd bods on the train being distributed amongst ten hotels. Our lorry stuck firm before long and showed every sign of going off the road, so we were pleased to finish the journey on foot. Our hotel – one of the smallest – is a chalet style place, rather suggesting that the front will open any time and a cuckoo will emerge with a mechanical whirr. It's sparsely furnished, but centrally heated and scrubbed spotlessly clean. Food's pretty simple, based on ordinary Army rations, but supplemented with such items as bacon and new laid egg every single morning.

The little village of Ehrwald itself lies in a sort of basin ringed round with magnificent peaks, dotted on the lower slopes of which are beautiful little houses and pine trees, all looking as though there's marzipan icing and rich fruit cake underneath the floorboards. The village is dominated by one mountain in particular – the highest in Germany and Austria I believe – called the The Zugspitze. Climbing is impossible in this season, but there's a cable railway to the summit which we may sample during our stay. Needless to say the whole place – from mountain peaks to the Austrian babies being pushed round in prams fitted with skis in place of wheels – just asks to be photographed.

On the afternoon of our arrival we were fitted out with skis, boots and snowsuits and assigned to Austrian instructors in classes of about ten or twelve. The instructors, of course, fill one with envy at their ability, but – thanks to their infinite patience and barring such accidents as a sprained knee or ankle – I have high hopes that Joyce and I will be at least become competent skiers by the end of our stay here … we can hit a fair speed down a slope … though I won't deny we've had to brush a lot of snow off ourselves since Monday!

Hiring a small German bus and waiting at Brennersee

The Italian frontier

Dear Dad   *12.xii.47*

Have had a most interesting day today – last night I fell in with a British Red Cross man – quite crazy – who wanted to go to Italy. Now Ehrwald lies at the junction of the American Zone of Germany and the French Zone of Austria, and the British only have a leave centre here by a special concession: so all travelling save on our Special train across the frontiers is 'verboten'. But this chap was so keen that he, Joyce, I and a couple of ATS officers chartered a small German bus for a few dozen cigarettes and set out early this morning. The bus driver took us to Innsbruck, through some wonderful mountains on a horribly icy road. He wouldn't go any further because of the petrol shortage, but dumped us there. Innsbruck is a quaint place (or was, before the Lancasters noticed it) – a full size city dumped down in the shade of the most terrific mountains. From there we boarded the Milan express – without any tickets, movement orders or anything else! When the inspector came round I gave him four cigarettes and showed him all the old papers which have accumulated in my pockets in recent months. He let us remain on the train till we reached a little village called Steinach, on the edge of Austria, where we had coffee and our sandwiches. Then we found a little electric train which took us right down the Brenner Pass – a wonderful run – and deposited us on the Station frontier – still on the basis of an 'Authorisation Form for Ambulance Transport to Hamburg' and my identity card! We walked across the frontier, and had a chat with the scruffiest collection of station sentries you ever saw, and all duly 'set foot inside Italy'. Then we reversed the process and got back home just about twelve hours after we set out. So I can now claim to have 'been in' France, Andorra, Belgium, Holland, Germany, Austria and Italy!

Saturday, 13 December

Very cloudy all day – J's 25th birthday. Last night I gave her a small book on Cambridge as a present. We went skiing this morning as usual, though the class that we've just begun to know is breaking up since many of its members have to return today. Notably we're losing L/Cpl Brown, a jovial, fat ATS girl who is one of the most spontaneous humourists I've met.

This afternoon the new arrivals were being fitted out with skis, so in the absence of our instructor, J and I did a little practise on our own. Then had a prowl round the village and plonked down another £1 to cover the loan of our equipment for the remainder

of our stay. Long talk in the 'lounge' with our new fellow guests and a short session in the NAAFI with Young ('Salvation Yeo'). Had yesterday's films developed locally – all successful shots but feel rather disgruntled because some careless handling has scratched the film.

The parish Church of Maria Heimsuchung (1648) Ehrwald

Sunday, 14 December

No organised instruction today – I went out this morning and this afternoon and practised on my own on the slopes outside our Pension. After dinner tonight went down to the NAAFI for supper. Had to listen to much binding today from a wife staying here who is disappointed because 'there's nothing to do at night' and 'no organised trips' – apparently quite oblivious to the privileges attendant upon just seeing Ehrwald itself and absolutely incapable of creating amusement for herself. In the same class is an ATS officer who grumbles because the ex-Olympic skier who teaches us does not speak perfect English – neither the thought that no one else has failed to progress under his tuition or that she might try learning German – has occurred to her.

Monday, 15 December

This morning we were assigned a fresh instructor, pleasant youth of about twenty who prefaces each remark with 'Hello' – apparently his only English expletive. Under his guidance did more snow ploughing and turning and tonight did our fastest and longest descent to date – at the conclusion of which J unfortunately sat down so firmly as to incapacitate her for a short time! In other respects, however, her prowess at turning etc. now exceeds mine! Evening spent in the NAAFI with chips and custard cream along the now usual lines!

Church of Maria Heimsuchung

Tuesday, 16 December
Tonight we went to a Tyrolean concert at the NAAFI – attractive, colourful, traditional costumes, some lusty yodelling and amusing 'Schuhplattler' dances – done to the rhythm of hands clapped on shoes and leather pantaloons. Particularly good was a woodcutting dance done to the rhythm of axes hacking flying splinters out of a pine log. Altogether a novel and entertaining evening.

Dear Dad   *Tuesy. 12.xii.47*

There is little doubt in my mind that the money put into Ehrwald and the other winter sports centres by the War Office, is not spent from purely altruistic motives – all the skiing that goes on receives marked official approbation, and no expense seems to have been spared in getting the best possible instructors – most of those here are ex-Olympic team members. Special Army classes are being set up, and it seems that the powers-that-be have got their eye on a possible need for Mountain Warfare units.

Off in a couple of hours – had some really fast skiing this morning.

Cocoa from the sledge in the middle of the morning

Pipe as smoked in Tyrol with a porcelain bowl

Wednesday, 17 December
Up at 08.30 hrs for the ski races which marked our last complete day here. What little hope we had of distinguishing ourselves, however, vanished when we were assigned to the 'Advanced Beginners' class. We tramped a great distance up the ski slopes – the males higher than the females – and started down a long, tortuous route at timed intervals. Since mensuration was by ordinary wristwatches at each end of the course, inaccuracies were inevitable. Anyhow my ski came off at the first corner and put me out of the running – once I got it securely fastened, however, I ran down fairly well and enjoyed it. More practice this afternoon, and tonight a dance at the NAAFI, where certificates were presented to the winners ... some obviously in incorrect classes! We tried to entertain Harti, our instructor, but he was shy, embarrassed and handicapped by the deficiencies of his English. Anyhow he had to leave because his girlfriend was waiting for him. Home, packed and to bed.

Thursday, 18 December
This morning we went skiing for the last time – doing stem turns on a sharp slope – I had my most successful session to date and felt, by the time I handed the skis in this afternoon, that I'd really made some progress in this business.

Rest of the day devoted to packing, reading and hanging about waiting for the lorry to take us to the train. When it came it got bogged down in the snow and a second one took us to the train just on 20.00 hrs.

Had a good dinner, found an empty compartment and, at about 23.00 hrs, settled down on the seat. Night rather marred by a sharp fall of temperature at about 04.00 hrs, but on the whole I was fairly comfortable.

Friday, 19 December
Breakfast at 09.00 hrs and then read whilst J prattled with some children until 11.30 hrs, when we had an early lunch. Train reached Hannover just before 13.00 hrs – the rest of Germany we find has had a light snowfall during recent days ... Went up to SSQ to collect my mail – nothing startling has happened in my absence, but Sgt Williams has secured a postponement, indefinitely, of his posting.

The village of Ehrwald

Saturday, 20 December

Back to work this morning – but not a lot to do in SSQ. Collected odd parcels, posted letters etc. This afternoon went shopping with J. This evening listened to *Ten Minute Alibi* on Radio Theatre and almost immediately after retired to bed.

Sunday, 21 December

Up at 11.00 hrs – two hours' work this morning; subsequently wrote several letters and posted some more of our holiday snaps. Up to see the prisoners and collect my mail. After dinner went out to hear a concert, under the impression that it was going to consist largely of excerpts from operas. Actually the Hamburg Symphony Orchestra changed its programme and played Beethoven's V Symphony instead, to my dismay.

Home in time to hear *Scrapbook for 1912* and so to bed.

Dear Dad   *Mony. 22.xii.47*

Preparations for the festive season now proceeding apace – I've ordered a turkey, a slab of pork. We have some Xmas puddings and Joyce has made and iced a magnificent fruit cake and this weekend has been experimenting with mincemeat. I've bought five cigars and extracted the boiled sweets from various time-expired emergency packs. It only remains to adjust our 'rum' issues now to ensure adequate flavouring and ignition of the Plum Pud.

Wednesday, 24 December
XMAS EVE
Very light morning's work today, and we finished completely at lunchtime. Stayed in SSQ until about 15.00 hrs talking etc., then – collecting the sundries I'd purchased from the PSI this morning – returned home. Alex arrived from Wolfenbüttel about 17.00 hrs and we all had dinner before going out to the YMCA to ring up Daventry and Mill Hill – after a slight delay I was able to speak to Dad, Alice, Pam and Grace. Whilst on the Daventry line we were fortunate in finding both of J's parents at home.

Returned to the flat but had to go out to see a man found drunk – feeling deliberate and sadistic I gave him 1/10 gm Apomorphine i.v.i. The subsequent vomiting was dramatic in its rapidity but was not very productive.

To bed – when the Xmas tree had been decorated and Joyce's presents laid out before our respective pillow cases – at about 14.30 hrs.

Thursday, 25 December
CHRISTMAS DAY
Up fairly early – about 10.00 hrs – and opened all our parcels, myself conscious of the discrepancy between this Xmas Day and my solitary, pointless day last year. And, it must be admitted, a little of the excitement of my childhood years as I disclosed the gifts of books, calendar, pipe, tobacco etc.

Went up to SSQ alone, leaving J and Alex to go to the Colliers. Here we had a Xmas

Christmas Day at SSQ

The man in the dark jacket is a German orderly, while the RAF NCOs have festive ties (inset)

dinner with the German staff – perhaps not as good, or as hilarious as last year when we had all the 'old hands' and not Sgt Williams.

When the dinner was over, F/Lt Kirkland, the DO, who had also been present, accompanied me to the Colliers where we stayed until we all returned home.

Trudie arrived soon after, and at 21.40 hrs I sat down to the first Xmas dinner at my own table – a pair of chickens, some roast pork, cider, a magnificent pudding – the first Joyce has ever made – with Rum Sauce (made from issue rum!) followed by coffee, cherry brandy and a good cigar. The remainder of the night unfortunately was not terribly convivial – we listened to a poor radio play, conversation tended to lag, and only after Trudie had gone home and we talked about marriage did we work up for a short time a cheerful Xmas atmosphere. To bed at 04.00 hours.

Christmas Day with Alex and the Collier family

Christmas dinner at the flat with Alex, Kirkland, Trudie and Joyce

Saturday, 27 December

Again rose late – had a couple of calls to make this morning, and this afternoon all useful labour was precluded by the descent upon us of Mrs Collier and five odd children. When they had gone, Alex, J and I spent the rest of the evening with the Sellhorns and came back to bed.

Sunday, 28 December

Did not get up till 12.15 hrs! Then spent a very idle sort of day – a visit to SSQ and, this afternoon, when Alex had returned to Wolfenbüttel, an hour or so spent writing letters. This evening listened to a tale on the radio about 'a minder who made good in spite of TB' and so coffee and to bed, feeling that four days holiday was about enough and, as usual, a bit depressed that Xmas was all over.

Dear Dad   Suny. 28.xii.47

We had a pretty quiet holiday – intermitted by the usual drunks as far as I was concerned. Alex arrived on Xmas Eve and had returned to his unit this afternoon – I'd sent an invitation to Bob Cocks but he was unable to avail himself of it. For the first time I carved my own bird – we had a pair of small chickens – and all Joyce's cooking, including her first plum pudding and an iced Xmas cake, was most gratifyingly successful.

Had a note from Tim today describing a lecture by Montgomery and his own demob. dinner – he still seems rather behindhand in receiving my own notes.

Well, it only remains to wish all at No 5 a very prosperous New Year – and one which will, I sincerely trust, see us all reunited before it is very far advanced.

Best wishes to you all,
Yours Aye, Dick

Dear Pam   Suny. 28.xii.47

Thank you very much for the pipe. It is a very good one and just right for me. I smoke it every night and have a think about you.

This is to say 'Many Happy Returns' to you – I have not got any present yet, because there is nothing in Lüneburg for Big Girls that go to school. But when I go to Hamburg I'll find something NICE! So just wait and SEE!

Your own old
Dick

"ANY SECONDS?"

Monday, 29 December

Had expected a rush of work today, but it was quieter even than a usual Monday; had time to write a couple of letters and came home to plunge quite deeply into about 2½ hrs work. At the end of which time we listened to a very good play – *The Show* by J. Galsworthy – about an inquest on a suicide.

Tuesday, 30 December

Up a little late, by virtue of a touch of bronchitis. To SSQ at 09.30 hrs and had as dull a day as usual. This afternoon the G/C sent for me for a discussion about VD measures – he is a quieter, less opinionated and rather less sure man than G/C Walker and not nearly so given to talking.

Then back to SSQ to have a minor row with Sgt Williams about giving waste food to the German boilermen.

Home, and did a good 2½ hrs work. Heavy snow last night has been accompanied by a marked fall of temperature, and in consequence I felt inclined to sit down for a quiet read rather than to do the photographic prints I had planned.

Wednesday, 31 December

Returned home for lunch, went out for a short walk in the town afterwards and then did a couple of hours work. Finished off the afternoon by printing some snaps.

After dinner Kirkland took us to the cinema to see James Mason in *The Upturned Glass* – a good story about a neurosurgeon crazed with the desire to revenge the murder of his love – a task he accomplishes in a singularly crude non-technical manner and follows up by suicide. The shortcomings of the plot as a thriller were more than made up for by the typical 'British' style of film-making and the authenticity of the technical background – in which respect the film paralleled *Green For Danger*.

Home and listened to a very good New Year programme, with continuity by Robert Donat. We saw 1948 in at 01.00 hrs current British time and drank a glass of ginger wine to 'Group 70' and we retired to bed about an hour later.

STADE 1948

The New Year, almost as cold as the previous one, found Dick and Joyce firmly established in the hierarchy of RAF Lüneburg. Rumours of being demobbed that Summer abounded. With renewed vigour the acquisition of surgical instruments accelerated and opportunities to see more of Germany arrived with new postings. The standard of photography improved and the diary entries continued.

In April 1948 a longer posting to RAF Stade to the West of Hamburg followed. This had been a Luftwaffe fighter station for the defence of Hamburg.

The MO and his wife were accommodated in the spacious house of their Luftwaffe antecedents. Some of the streets within the station still bearing the names that had by then become less fashionable.

Ex Luftwaffe Mess Stade

The spacious house of their Luftwaffe antecedents

Diary – Monday, 5 April 1948

The nine o'clock news suggests that Skirly Foulds and his ambulances in Berlin will be busy – a Viking of BEA was hit by a Russian fighter there today and crashed with the loss of 14 lives. Coming at a time when the railway dispute was beginning to sober down, this cannot but have a deleterious effect on subsequent negotiations.

Diary – Monday, 19 April 1948

F/O Foulds is back in Stade to collect his kit and he rang me up to give a few details of the Viking crash in which, as I anticipated, he played an important part. Says he was fired on as he approached the crash to remove the bodies. Am wondering if he will receive any official recognition of his services.

Dear Dad   *Tuey. 20.4.48*

If all goes according to plan the three of us, and the greater part of our personal belongings, will travel to Stade by road on Thursday. I am told that I will be there till the end of May, but I think that's rather conjectural … this particular station has been on the verge of packing up since first I came out. Anyhow, it is unlikely that I'll ever really get 'dug-in' in Lüneburg again (though the flat here remains in my name) because I hope to be released soon after my return.

Stade is, by all accounts, a very cheerful station – only 6 officers and 80 men – in nice country with a convivial CO: there's very little work for me, but a little more than you might imagine since my responsibilities include a bunch of CCG (Control Commission, Germany) families and the ammunition dumps at Hasendorf, nearby. I'm hoping for 5–6 weeks undisturbed swotting!

Foulds is likely to be permanently posted to Berlin – he has returned to Stade to collect his kit this week; and I am looking forward to a chat with him before he leaves. He tells me on the 'phone that he was the first RAF chap on the scene of the Viking crash and played a correspondingly large part in the enquiry … from the proceedings of which the fact that his ambulance was fired on has not been divulged. I suppose it's just possible that he may receive e.g. an MBE for his services in such an important affair.

The intensive de-Nazification of Germany has removed most of the evidence of the Third Reich, and one can travel hundreds of miles & never see a swastika now.
Here & there though, traces persist — the RAF unit at Stade has left a few names hanging as the Germans left them.

433 EDD
BAFO

Dear Dad   Friy. 23.4.48

Only to tell you that Joyce, her mother and myself have duly changed our quarters and
are now safely installed here at Stade. We had the usual chaotic 48 hours immediately
before leaving Lüneburg, trying to get our belongings sorted out – the majority were
forwarded here by lorry, some are in storage at 1BR&SO and the less valuable stuff has
been left in the flat, to which we hope to return before long.

Had a pleasant drive over here – certainly Stade is situated in country which is much
more attractive than Lüneburg – more hills, more trees and less dust. There's a very
well equipped Sick Quarters here, with one orderly and no work … or at least a
negligible quantity.

The buildings are of the stereotyped German Air Force variety with which I am
becoming familiar – once a fighter station for the defence of Hamburg, it hasn't ever
been quite the same since a daylight raid during the last weeks of the war. About
one in every three or four of its buildings is habitable, and the unit here now is
simply a collecting centre for the repair or destruction of surplus equipment which is
subsequently sold e.g. to foreign governments.

We have been given the best house we're likely to have for years to come – situated
on the station itself, in excellent condition but a little scantily furnished. There are
only a few officers here and, as is usual on these small units, everyone is very friendly
and cooperative. Against this must be set the fact that Stade itself is little more than a
village, that Hamburg is rather inaccessible and amusements correspondingly restricted.
The life of the station from now on is indeterminate – it may close down in the latter
half of May … or go on indefinitely.

Foulds was here when I arrived and left by air for Berlin – where he is now permanently posted – at lunch time today. He has given me a gruesome account of the difficulties he experienced in sorting out the 14 bodies from the Viking crash … he could only find two heads and one of those he had to turn an extinguisher on before he could pick it up! The machine blew up when it hit the ground … he didn't enjoy his flight up here because he says he kept on noticing little cabin fittings and pieces of upholstery in his Viking, from which, in the other one, he'd had to scrape off fragments of tissue!

No more from this end for now – going to have my afternoon tea!
Yours aye,
Dick

Stade was built in the expansion of about 1938. Göring was THE man in the Luftwaffe & his name, & that of von Richthofen, adorn the main roads. The one seen here is on a little patch of waste ground.

The 1948 Gatow Air Disaster
5 April 1948

The Gatow air disaster was a collision that occurred in mid-air in the airspace over Germany and instigated an international incident. The two aircraft which collided near RAF Gatow air base were a British European Airways Vickers VC.1B Viking and a Soviet Air Force Yakovlev Yak-3 fighter. None of the ten passengers and four crew on board the Viking survived, nor the Soviet pilot. Following this disaster there was a major diplomatic impasse between the United Kingdom and the United States on the one hand and on the other the Soviet Union. This disagreement exacerbated the distrust already apparent on the lead up to the Berlin Blockade, one of the first major international crises of the Cold War.

The bridge at Flensburg

The Island of Sylt

The Island of Sylt in the North Frisian Islands had become a leave and recreation resort for the British forces. The temporary posting as Medical Officer to the island resulted in Dick and Joyce taking up residence at the Viking Hotel for an extended period in June 1948. Besides the attractions of sea and sand, the aviation archaeology was fascinating. Scattered about the coast were heavy defences to protect the installations that housed the Luftwaffe's seaplanes. The demolition of the giant lifting cranes was witnessed and photographed and more traditional seaside holiday snaps pepper the archive.

Above: The demolition of the giant lifting cranes witnessed and photographed by RH. Joyce and RH (opposite) on the quay at Finkenwerder, near Stade. The centre white vessel is believed to be a German wartime Flugbetriebsboot (Air-Sea Rescue Launch) used to rescue ditched Luftwaffe aircrew.

The Return to the UK

The return to the UK and demobilisation eventually happened in July 1948. Not, however, before RH had had his first sight of a Jet fighter, a Vampire.

Diary – Friday, 2 July 1948

Rose at 10.00 hrs and proceeded to the Mess at lunch time, spending the afternoon furthering my clearance of the station. Spent all the evening until about nine o'clock continuing our packing.

This afternoon had my first chance to inspect a 'jet' at close quarters – a 'Vampire' here for servicing. Wrote a brief letter to Dad giving details of my return to the UK.

The process of packing the accumulated material of two years in Europe took several weeks. The packing cases, purpose made in the workshops of RAF Lüneburg, were carefully hand painted with his address before despatch. Mostly they contained quantities of surgical instruments and remained packed for the rest of Richard's life. The National Health Service commenced on 5 July 1948 and the need for doctors to provide their own tools vanished.

Diary – Tuesday, 6 July 1948

Our last day in Germany. Rose at 09.15 hrs and spent most of the morning on the 'Marching Out' inspection of our flat and arranging the transit of our remaining luggage to the airfield. Then went up with it and had lunch in the Mess before collecting my Movement Orders etc., and signing testimonials for the German staff.

Shook the dust of 'Airfield B.156' off my feet at 16.55 hrs and came home for a light tea. Trudie and her mother came round to say goodbye. We exchanged presents and then Joyce and I went to the cinema. *Brighton Rock* – a murder film in French style with some good photography but rather depressing in its sordidly relentless depiction of life of a race-course gang.

Home and stacked our formidable collection of personal luggage against the day which always seemed so remote – right up to now – when we finally leave Germany.

The diary entry for that journey across the North Sea remains.

Diary – Wednesday, 7 July 1948

Up at 05.45 hrs and left Lüneburg quite smoothly according to plan – a Volkswagen took us to the station at 07.00 hrs and the train steamed out at 07.30 hrs. Had a comfortable seat in a not overcrowded carriage, but even so felt pretty tired by the time the trip was over. I slept until we reached Hannover, but not much thereafter – we travelled via Minden, Bückeburg and Bad Oeynhausen. Then into the Ruhr via Bielefeld, Dortmund and Essen. Had dinner in the restaurant car as we passed through Arnhem and Bockum, having successfully negotiated a very cursory 'inspection' by a CCG official at the German frontier.

Went through the outskirts of Rotterdam – apparently a city of flats – and arrived at a very quiet but rather abandoned looking quay ('The Hook') at 21.00 hrs. There I changed our BAFSV [British Armed Forces Special Voucher] into Sterling, and J left me to take passage on the civilian packet. I was shepherded onto the military transport – rather a small boat, very full and with rather disappointing accommodation – folding metal-and-canvas bunks in tiers of three. Watched the ship cast off at 22.30 hrs, as it was growing dark, and then went down to the canteen for two cups of tea. The sea was very smooth, but the ship began to pitch a little in the middle of the night. By then I had hung up the Guppy fish I was carrying in a safe position and – nauseated by the day's travelling and an excess of tobacco rather than by the ship's motion, had taken 1/50 gm Hyoscine hydrobromide to be on the safe side and was soundly asleep.

No account remains of the reunion with family and friends the next day, Richard's birthday. We now rely on that provided by his brother Tim who had returned from Palestine and East Africa and was himself now demobbed.

"I left my office and travelled to Liverpool Street station to meet the Leave Train. The platform was deserted and the only figure of authority present was a RAF Police corporal, immaculately pressed and polished. When questioned as to the whereabouts of my brother he reported that the train had arrived early. 'I think I know the officer you mean, Sir, was he carrying some fish in a jar?'"

Postscript

Richard and Joyce were soon able to set up home in Stanmore. By 1950 another Richard had been added to the bloodline. In the Coronation Year a short notification appeared in the Births column of *The Times* to report that young Richard had a 'sparring partner', Peter. The small house must have been chaotic when Joyce coined the phrase 'your father is playing soldiers this weekend.' He'd been commissioned into 44 Para Field Ambulance, a highly trained Territorial Army airborne unit. Fellowship of the Royal College of Surgeons in May 1952 was followed by a succession of hospital posts. The diaries continued in a less detailed form. Occasionally his eye for describing disturbing events is again evident.

Diary – Tuesday, 17 October 1948

Whilst on my way home today via Mill Hill, the bus conductor described how he had seen a Dakota crash 10–15 minutes before on Highwood Hill. So I stayed on the bus and went up to find it just next door to Sellar's house. It had landed on its back and burnt up in a garden, after striking the trees and a brick wall. The pilot was lying clear of the debris, quite dead but there were no other corpses immediately evident. I introduced myself to the RAF officers present and had a look at the remains of the centre-section – I'd always been very curious as to my possible reactions to this sort of sight but I must be a little more inured than I'd thought, because I wasn't at all perturbed. Indeed I was mildly surprised at the squeamishness of the firemen, who all seemed to find it necessary to wear rather inefficient looking rubber gloves and to handle the corpse through the thickness of a blanket. Thought at first it was an RAF machine – then saw sanitary towels scattered all over the place and realised it was a BEA with 28 on board – plus 1 survivor who had already gone to hospital. Seems that it turned back to Northolt when one engine cut, and probably tried to force land because the other began to fail. Pilot probably in control throughout judging by line of flight and probably undershot the fields on Highwood Hill.

In 1963 Richard, Joyce and the boys moved to Ulverston in what is now termed Cumbria for his last professional advancement as Orthopædic Consultant in Barrow-in-Furness. His close association with Vickers Armstrong the ship builders soon provided the opportunity to go to sea on the proving trials of Her Majesty's latest ships, including

HMS *Mohawk* and the fated HMS *Sheffield*. The photographs were in colour by now, as were those of the Airborne Forces in training.

Joyce was fully occupied with the WI and the Embroiderers' Guild. In retirement Richard transferred his writing and photographic skills to non clinical Medico-Legal work. Inevitably he missed the milieu of a large hospital and continued to haunt the corridors whilst attending post-graduate lectures and seminars. Those corridors were probably where he contracted Swine Flu during the 2009 epidemic. A damaged heart valve took him to meet 'the sure physician' in December. He was buried on Joyce's birthday.

At the time of writing Joyce lives in a quiet residential care home in East Sussex. On her dressing table is a handcrafted wooden marquetry jewellery box containing her souvenirs from those days in Germany. Reading aloud the letters on the lid she nods thoughtfully, 'Lüneburg 1947. Good!'

think you will lik...

work and, with a warm

APPENDICES

APPENDIX 1
THE BOLLMAN CASE

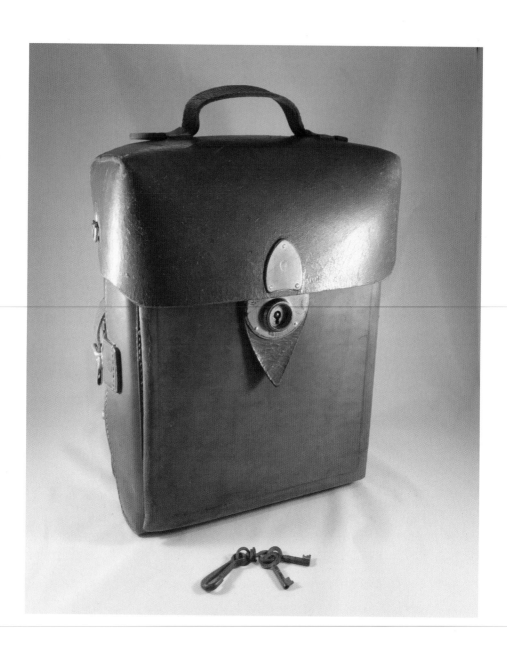

GERMAN ARMY SURGICAL KIT

Monday, 13 January 1947
"Today did a bit more 'Black' buying an ex German Army surgical case in lovely leather, for 250 cigarettes."

Seventy years later this item remains the best preserved and most interesting item of Richard Harrison's acquisitions from Germany. It appears never to have been issued and was certainly not used again in peacetime.

Date marked 1942, it was manufactured by the firm of Bollman in Tuttlingen. A set of keys open the hinged lid under which is fitted a ten piece set of surgical instruments by the firm of Aesculap. In fitted metal trays labelled Ampullen and Tabletten can be found glass ampoules, some labelled Garnison Lazarett (Garrison Hospital) Spandau.

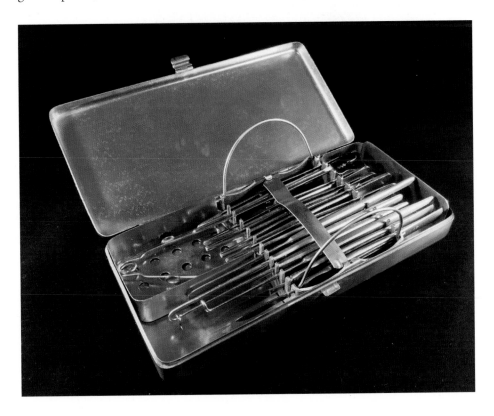

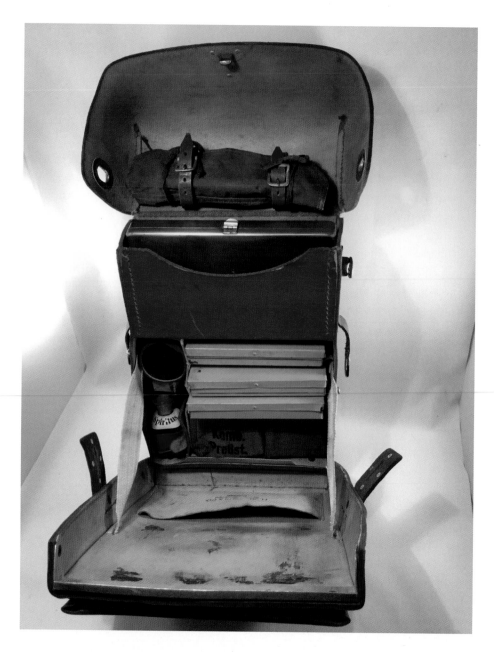

Also included are a rubber tourniquet bandage, spirit bottle, soap container, compressed bandages and a stapling device for wound closure as can be seen in the image on the opposite page.

The firm of Bollman (established in 1892) still exists as a manufacturer of surgical cases in the town of Tuttlingen. During World War 2 Bollman's supplied both surgical cases and stretchers to the German Army.

Today this town has 600 medical equipment manufacturers providing 50 per cent of the world's medical equipment.

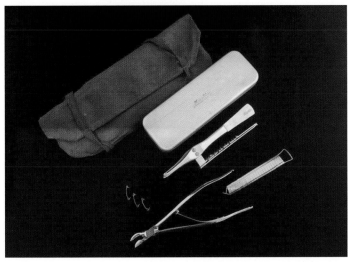

Left: Staple kit for skin closure manufactured by Martin (Tuttlingen) contained within an oilcloth pouch.

APPENDIX 2
FIREPOWER DISPLAY

A significant omission from Richard's diary in 1948 is any description of what was clearly a substantial firepower display mounted by elements of British armoured units, probably in Lüneburg, from the large ex-Wehrmacht Cavalry Barracks. RH's photographs are both interesting and dramatic.

Ford F60 with a single 40mm Bofors and a spare barrel

Churchill Crocodile flame-throwing tank, based on a Churchill Mark VII. It is probably serving with the Specialist Armour Establishment, formed from the remains of the 79th Armoured Division.

Ford F60L truck with a triple Polsten AA gun

Sexton self-propelled gun

A Cromwell IV or VI fitted with a 95mm Howitzer. Turret marking C Squadron probably from the 10th Hussars

From left to right: The front corner of a Sexton self-propelled gun, a Centurion Mark II, a Churchill (probably the Crocodile), a Cromwell IV or VI fitted with a 95mm Howitzer. The first truck is a Ford, next to it is a Morris and the last vehicle is a Daimler Armoured Car Mark II.

APPENDIX 3
RH'S AIRCRAFT PHOTOGRAPHY

TZ128 Spitfire XIV of 411 Squadron RCAF